D0571697

A Classic Nativity

DEVOTIONAL

A Classic Nativity DEVOTIONAL

compiled by
JAMES STUART BELL

Tyndale House Publishers, Inc.
Carol Stream, Illinois

Visit Tyndale's exciting Web site at www.tyndale.com

TYNDALE and Tyndale's quill logo are registered trademarks of Tyndale House Publishers, Inc.

A Classic Nativity Devotional

Designed by Jacqueline L. Noe

ISBN-13: 978-1-4143-1501-0
ISBN-10: 1-4143-1501-5

Printed in the United States of America

11 10 09 08 07 06
6 5 4 3 2 1

To Brendan Edward Bell,
a wise man
who continually seeks Him

Contents

Nativity Five: The Birth of Jesus Fulfills the Promises of God

Nativity Six: Humble Beginnings to Reach All of Humanity

Nativity Seven: Celebrate and Share the Good News of Christ's Birth

Acknowledgments

To the editorial team at Tyndale who helped with the challenging task of making this available for the Christmas season: Ken Petersen, Carol Traver, MaryLynn Layman, and David Lindstedt.

Luke Nativity Narration

From the Gospel according to Luke, chapter 2, verses 1–35

"In those days Caesar Augustus issued a decree that a census should be taken of the entire Roman world. (This was the first census that took place while Quirinius was governor of Syria.) And everyone went to his own town to register.

"So Joseph also went up from the town of Nazareth in Galilee to Judea, to Bethlehem the town of David, because he belonged to the house and line of David. He went there to register with Mary, who was pledged to be married to him and was expecting a child. While they were there, the time came for the baby to be born, and she gave birth to her firstborn, a son. She wrapped him in cloths and placed him in a manger, because there was no room for them in the inn.

"And there were shepherds living out in the fields nearby, keeping watch over their flocks at night. An angel of the Lord appeared to them, and the glory of the Lord shone around them, and they were terrified. But the angel said to them, 'Do not be afraid. I bring you good news of great joy that will be for all the people. Today in the town of David a Savior has been born to you; he is Christ the Lord. This will be a sign to you: You will find a baby wrapped in cloths and lying in a manger.'

"Suddenly a great company of the heavenly host appeared with the angel, praising God and saying, 'Glory to God in the highest, and on earth peace to men on whom his favor rests.'

"When the angels had left them and gone into heaven, the shepherds said to one another, 'Let's go to Bethlehem and see this thing that has happened, which the Lord has told us about.'

"So they hurried off and found Mary and Joseph, and the baby, who was lying in the manger. When they had seen him, they spread the word concerning what had been told them about this child, and all who heard it were amazed at what the shepherds said to them. But Mary treasured up all these things and pondered them in her heart. The shepherds returned, glorifying and praising God for all the things they had heard and seen, which were just as they had been told.

"On the eighth day, when it was time to circumcise him, he was named Jesus, the name the angel had given him before he had been conceived.

"When the time of their purification according to the Law of Moses had been completed, Joseph and Mary took him to Jerusalem to present him to the Lord (as it is written in the Law of the Lord, 'Every firstborn male is to be consecrated to the Lord'), and to offer a sacrifice in keeping with what is said in the Law of the Lord: 'a pair of doves or two young pigeons.'

"Now there was a man in Jerusalem called Simeon, who was righteous and devout. He was waiting for the consolation of Israel, and the Holy Spirit was upon him. It had been revealed to him by the Holy Spirit that he would not die before he had seen the Lord's Christ. Moved by the Spirit, he went into the temple courts. When the parents brought in the child Jesus to do for him what the custom of the Law required, Simeon took him in his arms and praised God, saying:

'Sovereign Lord, as you have promised,
you now dismiss your servant in peace.
For my eyes have seen your salvation,

which you have prepared in the sight of all people,
a light for revelation to the Gentiles
and for glory to your people Israel.'

"The child's father and mother marveled at what was said about him. Then Simeon blessed them and said to Mary, his mother: 'This child is destined to cause the falling and rising of many in Israel, and to be a sign that will be spoken against, so that the thoughts of many hearts will be revealed. And a sword will pierce your own soul too.'"

Because the Christmas service is the most frequently attended church service each year, this Scripture reading is probably the most familiar passage to Christians of all backgrounds and levels of commitment. It has a grace, beauty, and wonder to it that never grows stale. Nothing in all of creation, in all of history, can compare to this event—the beginning of God's perfect revelation to us in our very own form—a human being with all its limitations, yet God of very God. Let us kneel in worship and praise God for his lavish gift.

Introduction

On a quiet night two millennia ago in a tiny, peaceful village in the land we now know as Israel, an event took place that would profoundly and irrevocably change the course of the world as we know it.

That evening, some simple shepherds—young people who spent their time protecting valuable flocks of sheep from thieves, poachers, and wild animals—received the news. The stillness and solitude of the evening was suddenly and brilliantly broken by the terrifying yet spectacular sight and sound of an angel of God appearing to them with some incredible news. The angel's message, at first soothing but then astounding, went like this:

> "Do not be afraid. I bring you good news of great joy that will be for all the people. Today in the town of David a Savior has been born to you; he is Christ the Lord. This will be a sign to you: You will find a baby wrapped in cloths and lying in a manger."
>
> LUKE 2:10-12

This was the news these young people—as well as their Jewish brethren past and present—had so desperately and longingly waited for: The Messiah had come! After the Jewish people spent centuries waiting for their God to fulfill the promises he had made so long ago, the One they had all waited for had come.

There was nothing else they could do. "Let's go to Bethlehem and see this thing that has happened, which the Lord has told us about" (Luke 2:15). They did just that, and because they were willing to drop everything they were doing that night and travel to the town of Bethlehem, they saw for themselves—even became part of—what Christians have come to know as the original Nativity.

This is the event that was the beginning of what Christians know as the Incarnation, or as the apostle John put it, when "the Word became flesh and made his dwelling among us" (John 1:14).

Since that night, most of the Christian world has adopted as one of its annual celebrations the birth of our Savior, Jesus Christ. While the holiday that came to be known as "Christmas" has gone through countless twists and turns over the centuries—and while its origins are still a source of debate for some believers—it remains in the minds and lives of Christians a commemoration of an event that changed the world forever.

Christianity's past (as well as its present) is rich with tradition and writings surrounding the birth of Christ. In the few centuries following the death and resurrection of Jesus Christ, hundreds of years before Christmas became a holiday, the church fathers wrote passionately of the birth of Jesus and the events surrounding it, all of which they recognized as a spectacular example of the providence of God.

Since those early years of the Christian faith, believers of all shades and stripes of the faith have written and spoken about the birth of Christ—about the announcements of angels, about the young virgin girl chosen of God to be his mother, about Joseph her betrothed, about their trip to the town of Bethlehem, and about the visits of shepherds and magi from the east.

That work continues to this very day, and it includes the motion picture *The Nativity Story*, which opens worldwide in December 2006 and provides the inspiration for this book.

This book is a collection of writings—sermons, prose, poems, and hymns—all written to commemorate the day God appeared on earth as a man, the day our Savior was born. It includes works of early church fathers (the first four or so centuries following Jesus' death, resurrection, and ascension back to heaven), of leading Catholics throughout the centuries, of Orthodox sources, and of Protestant sources. Some of the names are well-known, and some are more obscure.

What these writings have in common, as diverse as their sources may be, is this: They express wonder at a God who loved humanity so much that he humbled his own Son by allowing him not only to be born of a virgin, but to be born in the meanest of circumstances.

The purpose of this book is to help you share in the wonderment of those long-ago events and what they mean to you personally. It's to get you to understand the profound love of a God who saw the fallen, wicked, hurting condition of humanity as a whole and said, "I'll go to save them myself." It is to get you to look upon the birth of Jesus Christ with the same amazement as a man named John Chrysostom, the "Golden-Mouthed" preacher/church father from the fourth and fifth centuries, who once exclaimed,

> I behold a new and wondrous mystery! My ears resound to the shepherd's song, piping no soft melody, but loudly chanting a heavenly hymn! The angels sing! The archangels blend their voices in harmony! The cherubim resound their joyful praise! The Seraphim exalt His glory!
>
> All join to praise this holy feast, beholding the Godhead here on earth, and man in heaven. He who is above now, for our salvation, dwells here below; and we, who were lowly, are exalted by divine mercy! Today Bethlehem

> resembles heaven, hearing from the stars the singing of angelic voices and, in place of the sun, witnessing the rising of the Sun of Justice!

So read and enjoy. Read not just during what we have come to know as the Christmas season but also during those times when you need to rekindle your gratefulness and astonishment at the arrival of our Lord into this world.

NATIVITY ONE

God's Loving Gift

In the Bleak Midwinter

In the bleak midwinter
Frosty wind made moan,
Earth stood hard as iron,
Water like a stone;
Snow had fallen, snow on snow,
Snow on snow,
In the bleak midwinter,
Long ago.

Our God, Heaven cannot hold Him
Nor earth sustain;
Heaven and earth shall flee away
When He comes to reign.
In the bleak midwinter
A stable-place sufficed
The Lord God Almighty,
Jesus Christ.

Enough for Him, Whom cherubim
Worship night and day,
Breastful of milk
And a mangerful of hay;
Enough for Him, Whom angels

Fall before,
The ox and ass and camel
Which adore.

Angels and archangels
May have gathered there,
Cherubim and seraphim
Thronged the air,
But His mother only,
In her maiden bliss,
Worshipped the beloved
With a kiss.

What can I give Him,
Poor as I am?
If I were a shepherd
I would bring a lamb,
If I were a Wise Man
I would do my part;
Yet what I can I give Him:
Give my heart.

—Christina Rossetti (1830–1882)

There is nothing we can give God to repay him for the gift of his Son, Jesus Christ. But what we can do is give to him what he came to claim for himself in the first place: our hearts. God has already given us the greatest Christmas gift in history. All he wants in return is all that we are.

Christ's Nativity: God's Gift Just for Us

Adapted from a sermon by John Wycliffe (1324–1384)

For to us a child is born, to us a son is given,
and the government will be on his shoulders. And he
will be called Wonderful Counselor, Mighty God,
Everlasting Father, Prince of Peace.

ISAIAH 9:6

According to the joy the Bible reveals, we may say on Christmas Day that a child is born to us—for we believe that Jesus Christ was born on this day. It is God's spoken and written Word that tells us, both in figure and in letter, that a child is born to us, and it is in him that we should have this joy. And three short words are to be spoken from Isaiah's speech so that men may afterward joy in the service of this child.

First, we believe that since our first elders had sinned, there must be satisfaction made by the righteousness of God. For as God is merciful, so is he full of righteousness. But how should he judge all the world unless he kept righteousness in it? For the Lord against whom this sin was done is God almighty; and no sin may be done except against God. And the greater the Lord is against whom the sin is done, the more is that sin to be punished by this Lord. It would be a great sin to act against the king's bidding; but that sin which is done against God's bidding would be even more without excuse.

According to our belief, God told Adam not to eat of the fruit. But he broke God's command, and he was not excused in that sin, neither by his own folly (or weakness), nor by Eve, nor by the serpent. And so by the righteousness of God this sin must always be punished. And it is a light word to say that God must of his power forgive this sin without the justification that was made for this trespass. For God might do this if he would; but his justice will not permit anything else except that each trespass must be punished, either on earth or in hell. And God may not accept a person, and forget his sin, without satisfaction—else he must give men and angels free permission to sin. And then sin were no sin, and our God were no god. And this is the first lesson that we take from our faith.

The second teaching that we take is that he who should make satisfaction for the sin of our first father must be both God and man. For as mankind trespassed, so must mankind make satisfaction. And therefore it could not be that an angel should make satisfaction for man, for neither has he the right, nor was his the nature that sinned here. But since all men are one person, that person makes satisfaction for man, if any member of this person makes satisfaction for all of this person.

And in this way we see that if God made another man who was after the nature of Adam, he would be obligated to God as much as he might be for himself, and so he might not make satisfaction both for himself and for Adam's sins. And since satisfaction had to be made also for Adam's sin, as it is said, such a person that must make the satisfaction must be both God and man; for the worthiness of this person's deeds must be equal to the unworthiness of the sin.

The third teaching that must follow these two is that the child is born to man to make satisfaction for man's sin. And this child must be God and man, given to man. And he must bear his empire upon his shoulder and suffer for man. And this child is Jesus Christ, who we suppose was born today.

If we truly desire that this child be born to us, we have joy of this child, and we follow him in three virtues: in righteousness, and meekness, and patience for our God. For whoever condemns Christ unto his death, against the spirit, shall be condemned of this Child, even as all others shall be saved. And thus the joy of this child that was meek and full of virtues should make men to be little in malice. Then they observe well the season.

To them who will fight and chide, I say, to this child who is born as Prince of Peace, and loves peace; and condemns contrary men, who are contrary to peace. For we study how Christ came in the fullness of time when he should; and how he came in meekness, as his birth teaches us; and how he came in patience from his birth to his death; and we follow him in these three because of the joy that we have in him. For this joy, in this patience of Christ, brings us to a joy that shall last forever.

Jesus Christ came to earth two thousand years ago—born as an ordinary infant but still possessing all the attributes and character of divinity—as God's gift to a needy, sinful, lost humankind. It was our sin that made it necessary for him to come, but it was our heavenly Father's incredible grace, mercy, and love that made the event possible.

On the Morning of Christ's Nativity

This is the month, and this the happy morn
Wherein the Son of Heav'n's eternal King,
Of wedded Maid, and Virgin Mother born,
Our great redemption from above did bring;
For so the holy sages once did sing,
That he our deadly forfeit should release,
And with his Father work us a perpetual peace.

That glorious Form, that Light unsufferable,
And that far-beaming blaze of Majesty,
Wherewith he wont at Heav'n's high council-table,
To sit the midst of Trinal Unity,
He laid aside, and here with us to be,
Forsook the courts of everlasting day,
And chose with us a darksome house of mortal clay.

Say Heav'nly Muse, shall not thy sacred vein
Afford a present to the Infant God?
Hast thou no verse, no hymn, or solemn strain,
To welcome him to this his new abode,
Now while the heav'n, by the Sun's team untrod,
Hath took no print of the approaching light,
And all the spangled host keep watch in squadrons bright?

See how from far upon the eastern road
The star-led wizards haste with odours sweet:
O run, prevent them with thy humble ode,
And lay it lowly at his blessed feet;
Have thou the honour first thy Lord to greet,
And join thy voice unto the angel quire,
From out his secret altar touched with hallowed fire.

—John Milton (1608–1674)

On the morning when we celebrate the scene known as the Nativity, we celebrate the day that Jesus Christ—the one and only begotten Son of the everlasting God—was born. It is the day Jesus left everything in heaven behind and came to earth to become one of us!

Our Savior's Humble Birth

Adapted from a sermon by the Reverend Alfred Barratt

When Jesus Christ was born in Bethlehem he did not have a Christmas tree. The children born in those days were not as fortunate as children of today. The parents of Jesus were very poor. His house was not a palace, but a stable; his bed was not a pretty cot with a silk floss mattress, but a manger filled with hay.

And yet in spite of his poverty and humility he was the only begotten Son of God, who left his throne in heaven above and came to earth in human form to live among the sin-bound people of this world to teach them the love of God and to show them how much love God has for us.

On the day of his birth, the heavenly choir of angels gave a grand concert in Bethlehem. They sang their sky-born carols away up in the sky over the place where the lowly Child Jesus lay cradled in a humble cattle shed. One of the most beautiful songs the angels sang on that never-to-be-forgotten day was "Glory to God in the highest, and on earth peace, good will toward men."

It must have been grand for those shepherds who were "abiding in the field, keeping watch over their flock by night" to hear such beautiful singing. But they did not celebrate this wonderful event by gathering around a Christmas tree. They just left their sheep and went down into Bethlehem to seek the newborn King, and when they found him they worshiped him.

The idea of a Christmas tree was not thought of in those days. The first Christmas tree was originated 732 years after the birth of Jesus Christ. Perhaps the children who were looking anxiously and with joy and great expectation to see the Christmas tree may like to hear the legend of the first Christmas tree. Yet it may not merely be a legend, but history sending forth its radiant light through the dreary mists of traditions.

It is an old German story—that Saint Wilfred transformed the heathen Teuton worship in the forest in the Christmas ceremony. About 732 years after the birth of Jesus Christ, he took a band of priests with him and sought to convert the worshipers of Thor. It was on Christmas Eve, while they were fighting their way through the deep snow in the dense forest, that they came upon a savage tribe assembled under a thick oak tree, which was symbolic of the god of thunder, Thor. The old, white-haired priest of the tribe was about to offer as a sacrifice to Thor the young, beautiful son of the tribe's chief. When Wilfred saw it he rushed forward and warded off the arm that was about to slay the child. The tribesmen were all delighted at the saving of their favorite, and because of this act they very soon became converts to Christianity. Saint Wilfred then took his ax and started to cut down the old oak tree. As it was about to fall, lightning struck it and rended it into many pieces, and in its place there sprang up a little fir tree, green and sparkling. They carried this little fir tree to the chief captain's hall, and set it in the middle of the room and round it they all made merry. It was about this first Christmas tree that the old, old story of Jesus and his love was told to the Teuton tribes, and in a short time they all became Christians.

Let us not forget that Christmas is the birthday of Jesus, and while we gather around the Christmas tree let us give our little hearts to Jesus as a Christmas present. He says today, "Give me your heart." If you will do this, he will give you in return a new sense of joy and peace that will not only shine through the Christmas season, but will remain with you throughout your earthly life. This would be a very fitting time to give your heart to Jesus, while the angels are singing again the Bethlehem anthem, "Glory to God in the highest, and on earth peace, good will toward men." Will you do this for your own sake, and for Jesus' sake?

Jesus humbled himself to come to earth and be born in the humblest of circumstances so we could know the heavenly Father who sent him in the first place. There is only one thing we can give him in return for this act of love and generosity, and that's our hearts.

Keeping Christmas

There is a better thing than the observance of Christmas day, and that is keeping Christmas.

Are you willing . . .

- to forget what you have done for other people, and to remember what other people have done for you;
- to ignore what the world owes you, and to think what you owe the world;
- to put your rights in the background, and your duties in the middle distance, and your chances to do a little more than your duty in the foreground;
- to see that men and women are just as real as you are, and try to look behind their faces to their hearts, hungry for joy;
- to own up to the fact that probably the only good reason for your existence is not what you are going to get out of life, but what you are going to give to life;
- to close your book of complaints against the management of the universe, and look around you for a place where you can sow a few seeds of happiness?

Are you willing to do these things even for a day? Then you can keep Christmas.

Are you willing . . .

- to stoop down and consider the needs and desires of little children;
- to remember the weakness and loneliness of people growing old;
- to stop asking how much your friends love you, and ask yourself whether you love them enough;
- to bear in mind the things that other people have to bear in their hearts;
- to try to understand what those who live in the same home with you really want, without waiting for them to tell you;
- to trim your lamp so that it will give more light and less smoke, and to carry it in front so that your shadow will fall behind you;
- to make a grave for your ugly thoughts, and a garden for your kindly feelings, with the gate open?

Are you willing to do these things, even for a day? Then you can keep Christmas.

Are you willing . . .

- to believe that love is the strongest thing in the world—
- stronger than hate, stronger than evil, stronger than death—
- and that the blessed life which began in Bethlehem

nineteen hundred years ago is the image and brightness of the Eternal Love?

Then you can keep Christmas.
And if you can keep it for a day, why not always?
But you can never keep it alone.

—HENRY VAN DYKE (1852–1933)

The scene we have come to know as the Nativity is a reminder to us of God's greatest gift to humankind: his Son, Jesus Christ, the long-awaited Savior coming to earth to be born as a baby and live as a human being. But it also serves as a reminder that Christmas is about remembering to give of ourselves much the way Jesus gives to us.

The Joy of the Nativity

Based on a sermon by Saint Augustine of Hippo (354–430)

Hear, O sons of light, who have been received by adoption into the kingdom of God; hear, my very dear brethren; hear and be glad in the Lord, ye just ones, so that praise may become the upright. Hear what you already know; reflect upon what you have heard; love what you believe; proclaim what you love.

Since we are celebrating a great anniversary on this day, you may expect a sermon in keeping with the feast. Christ as God was born of His Father, as Man of His Mother; of the immortality of His Father, of the virginity of His Mother; of His Father without a mother, of His Mother without a father; of His Father without limits of time, of His Mother without seed; of His Father as the source of life, of His Mother as the end of death; of His Father ordering all days, of His Mother consecrating this particular day.

God sent John to earth as His human Precursor so that he was born when the days were becoming shorter while the Lord Himself was born when the days were growing longer, that in this minute detail the subsequent words of this same John might be prefigured: "He must increase, but I must decrease" (John 3:30, KJV). For human life ought to grow weaker in itself and stronger in Christ, that "they who are alive may live no longer for themselves, but for him who died for all and rose again," and that each one of us may say in the words of the apostle: "I no longer live, but Christ lives in me" (Galatians 2:20). For "he must increase, but I must decrease."

All His angels worthily praise Him, for He is their everlasting food, nourishing them with an incorruptible feast. He is the Word of God, by whose life they live, by whose eternity they live forever, by whose goodness they live happily forever. They praise Him worthily, as God with God, and they render glory to God on high. May we, "the people of his pasture and the sheep of his hand" (Psalm 95:7, KJV), reconciled to Him by our good will, merit peace in consideration of the limited measure of our weakness. For these words to which the angels themselves gave utterance in jubilation at the birth of our Savior are their daily tribute: "Glory to God in the highest, and on earth peace, good will toward men" (Luke 2:14, KJV).

Therefore, they praise Him duly: let us praise Him in obedience. They are His messengers; we, His sheep. He filled their table in heaven; He filled our manger on earth. He is the fullness of their table because "in the beginning was the Word, and the Word was with God, and the Word was God" (John 1:1). He is the fullness of our manger because "the Word was made flesh, and dwelt among us" (John 1:14, KJV). So that man might eat the Bread of angels the Creator of the angels became man. The angels praise Him by living; we, by believing; they by enjoying, we by seeking; they by obtaining, we by striving to obtain; they by entering, we by knocking.

What human being could know all the treasures of wisdom and knowledge hidden in Christ and concealed under the poverty of His humanity? For, "though he was rich, yet for your sakes he became poor, so that you through his poverty might become rich" (2 Corinthians 8:9). When He assumed our mortality and overcame death, He manifested Himself in poverty, but He promised riches though they might be deferred; He did not lose them as if they were taken from Him. How great is the multitude of His sweetness which He hides from those who fear Him but which He reveals to those that hope in Him! For we understand only in part until that which is perfect comes to us. To make us worthy of this perfect gift, He, equal to the Father in the form of God, became like us in the form of a servant, and refashions us into the likeness of God. The only Son of God, having become the Son of Man, makes many sons of men the sons of God; and on these men, reared as servants, with the visible form of servants, He bestows the freedom of beholding the form of God. For "we are children of God, and what we will be has not yet been made known. But we know that when he appears, we shall be like him, for we shall see him as he is" (1 John 3:2).

What, then, are those treasures of wisdom and knowledge? What are those divine riches unless they be that which satisfies our longing? And what is that multitude of sweetness unless it be what fills us? "Show us the Father and that will be enough for us" (John 14:8). Furthermore, in one of the psalms, one of our race, either in our name or for our sake, said to Him, "I will be satisfied with seeing your likeness" (Psalm 17:15). But He and the Father are one, and the person who sees Him sees the Father also (see John 10:30,

14:9); therefore, "the LORD Almighty—he is the King of glory" (Psalm 24:10). Turning to us, He will show us His face and "that we may be saved" (Psalm 80:3); we shall be satisfied, and He will be sufficient for us.Therefore, let our heart speak thus to Him: "Your face, LORD, I will seek. Do not hide your face from me" (Psalm 27:8-9). And let Him reply to the plea of our hearts: "Whoever has my commands and obeys them, he is the one who loves me. He who loves me will be loved by my Father, and I too will love him and show myself to him" (John 14:21). Indeed, those to whom He addressed these words did see Him with their eyes; they heard the sound of His voice with their ears; they regarded Him as a man in their human heart. But, what eye has not seen, what ear has not heard, and what has not entered into the heart of man He promised to show to those who love Him (see 1 Corinthians 2:9-10).

Until this favor is granted to us, until He shows us what will completely satisfy us, until we drink to satiety of that fountain of life, while we wander about, apart from Him but strong in faith, while we hunger and thirst for justice, longing with an unspeakable desire for the beautiful vision of God, let us celebrate with fervent devotion His birthday in the form of a servant. Since we cannot, as yet, understand that He was begotten by the Father before the day-star, let us celebrate His birth of the Virgin in the nocturnal hours. Since we do not comprehend how His name existed before the light of the sun, let us recognize His tabernacle placed in the sun. Since we do not, as yet, gaze upon the Son inseparably united with His Father, let us remember Him as the "bridegroom coming out of his bride-chamber." Since we are not yet ready for the banquet of our Father, let us grow familiar with the manger of our Lord Jesus Christ.

The biblical account of Jesus' birth and the events leading up to it are only the beginning of what we learn about him as we grow in our relationship with him and become more like him every day.

The Three Kings

Three Kings came riding from far away,
Melchior and Gaspar and Baltasar;
Three Wise Men out of the East were they,
And they traveled by night and they slept by day,
For their guide was a beautiful, wonderful star.

The star was so beautiful, large and clear,
That all the other stars of the sky
Became a white mist in the atmosphere,
And by this they knew that the coming was near
Of the Prince foretold in the prophecy.

Three caskets they bore on their saddle-bows,
Three caskets of gold with golden keys;
Their robes were of crimson silk with rows
Of bells and pomegranates and furbelows,
Their turbans like blossoming almond-trees.

And so the Three Kings rode into the West,
Through the dusk of the night, over hill and dell,
And sometimes they nodded with beard on breast,
And sometimes talked, as they paused to rest,
With the people they met at some wayside well.

"Of the child that is born," said Baltasar,
"Good people, I pray you, tell us the news;
For we in the East have seen his star,
And have ridden fast, and have ridden far,
To find and worship the King of the Jews."

And the people answered, "You ask in vain;
We know of no King but Herod the Great!"
They thought the Wise Men were men insane,
As they spurred their horses across the plain,
Like riders in haste, who cannot wait.

And when they came to Jerusalem,
Herod the Great, who had heard this thing,
Sent for the Wise Men and questioned them;
And said, "Go down unto Bethlehem,
And bring me tidings of this new king."

So they rode away; and the star stood still,
The only one in the grey of morn;
Yes, it stopped—it stood still of its own free will,
Right over Bethlehem on the hill,
The city of David, where Christ was born.

And the Three Kings rode through the gate
and the guard,
Through the silent street, till their horses turned
And neighed as they entered the great inn-yard;
But the windows were closed, and the doors
were barred,
And only a light in the stable burned.

And cradled there in the scented hay,
In the air made sweet by the breath of kine,
The little child in the manger lay,
The child, that would be king one day
Of a kingdom not human, but divine.

His mother Mary of Nazareth
Sat watching beside his place of rest,
Watching the even flow of his breath,
For the joy of life and the terror of death
Were mingled together in her breast.

They laid their offerings at his feet:
The gold was their tribute to a King,
The frankincense, with its odor sweet,
Was for the Priest, the Paraclete,
The myrrh for the body's burying.

And the mother wondered and bowed her head,
And sat as still as a statue of stone;
Her heart was troubled yet comforted,
Remembering what the Angel had said
Of an endless reign and of David's throne.

Then the Kings rode out of the city gate,
With a clatter of hoofs in proud array;
But they went not back to Herod the Great,
For they knew his malice and feared his hate,
And returned to their homes by another way.

—Henry Wadsworth Longfellow (1807–1882)

Every element of the story of Christ's Nativity shows us that his arrival was orchestrated by a heavenly Father who was in complete control. While there was a man—Herod the Great—who wanted more than anything to snuff out the King before he could get his Kingdom started, his Father in heaven would in no way allow harm to come to him.

Proclaiming God's Greatness

Adapted from the writings of Bede the Venerable (673–735)

"My soul glorifies the Lord and my spirit rejoices in God my Savior" (Luke 1:46-47). With these words Mary first acknowledges the special gifts she has been given. Then she recalls God's universal favors, bestowed unceasingly on the human race.

For he has been mindful
of the humble state of his servant.
From now on all generations will call me blessed,
for the Mighty One has done great things for me—
holy is his name.
His mercy extends to those who fear him,
from generation to generation.
He has performed mighty deeds with his arm;
he has scattered those who are proud in their
inmost thoughts.
He has brought down rulers from their thrones
but has lifted up the humble.
He has filled the hungry with good things
but has sent the rich away empty.
He has helped his servant Israel,

remembering to be merciful
to Abraham and his descendants forever,
even as he said to our fathers.

LUKE 1:48-55

When a man devotes all his thoughts to the praise and service of the Lord, he proclaims God's greatness. His observance of God's commands, moreover, shows that he has God's power and greatness always at heart. His spirit rejoices in God his savior and delights in the mere recollection of his creator who gives him hope for eternal salvation.

These words are often for all God's creations, but especially for the mother of Jesus. She alone was chosen, and she burned with spiritual love for the son she so joyously conceived. Above all other saints, she alone could truly rejoice in Jesus, her Savior, for she knew that he who was the source of eternal salvation would be born in time in her body, in one person both her own son and her Lord.

For the Mighty One has done great things for me—holy is his name. Mary attributes nothing to her own merits. She refers all her greatness to the gift of the one whose essence is power and whose nature is greatness, for he fills with greatness and strength the small and the weak who believe in him.

She did well to add "holy is his name," to warn those who heard, and indeed all who would receive his words, that they must believe and call upon his name. For they too could share in everlasting holiness and true salvation according to the words of the prophet: "And everyone who calls on the name of the LORD will be saved" (Joel 2:32). This is the name she spoke of earlier: *and my spirit rejoices in God my Savior.*

Therefore it is an excellent and fruitful custom of holy Church that we should sing Mary's hymn at the time of evening prayer. By meditating upon the incarnation, our devotion is kindled, and by remembering the example of the mother of Jesus, we are encouraged to lead a life of virtue. Such virtues are best achieved in the evening. We are weary after the day's work and worn out by our distractions. The time for rest is near, and our minds are ready for contemplation.

As we focus on and contemplate the Nativity—that wonderful scene where our Savior was born—and all the events surrounding it, we can't help but proclaim the greatness of a God who loved us so much that he gave us his only Son.

The Story behind "Silent Night"

If the church organ had not broken down and if the organist had not been able to strum a few chords on a guitar in an emergency, the loveliest Christmas carol of them all might never have been written.

Twenty-six-year-old Father Joseph Mohr, assistant priest at the newly erected Church of St. Nicholas in Oberndorf, in the Austrian Alps, was far from happy when his organist friend, Franz Gruber, told him that the pipe organ could not be used for the special Christmas Eve Mass scheduled for December 24, 1818. Although he trained the choir and played the organ at Arnsdorf as well as at Oberndorf, thirty-one-year-old Gruber had neither the talent nor the time to repair broken connections, restore shattered pipes, or replace worn-out bellows. While Father Mohr was not desperate, he was a bit peeved at the prospect of a Midnight Mass without the traditional organ music.

To relieve his tension, he bundled himself up in his warmest winter clothes and went visiting among his humble people. Shortly after arriving at the home of one of his faithful families, a new baby was born to the poor laborer and his wife. The pastor compared that event with the birth of the Christ Child centuries earlier, and, upon arriving home a few hours later, conquered his fatigue and weariness long enough to pen four simple stanzas describing the wonder and the majesty of the first Christmas. His initial stanza contained these beautiful lines:

Silent night, Holy night!
All is calm, All is bright
Round yon Virgin Mother and Child,
Holy Infant, so tender and mild;
Sleep in heavenly peace!
Sleep in heavenly peace!

When Gruber burst into the room a few moments later with the news that the organ was hopelessly beyond repair, Father Mohr handed him the slip of paper on which he had written the new stanzas. While the choir-master read them, the priest picked up a guitar in an adjoining room, and handed it to him, saying, "If we can't have the organ, at least we can have a new song. Try your hand at this."

The more Gruber protested, the stronger Mohr insisted. To quiet his friend, Gruber strummed a few simple chords on the guitar, and soon was humming an original melody that seemed to express the sentiments of the poem perfectly. At midnight the new carol was sung for the first time.

It might have remained there at Oberndorf had not Karl Mauracher come from the valley of Zillertal to repair the organ early in 1819. Mohr asked Gruber to play the new carol for the famous organ builder and repairman, when the job was finally completed, and Mauracher fell in love with it right away. About ten years later he felt that the four gifted Strasser children, Caroline, Joseph, Andreas, and Amalie, were just the ones to give the new song to the world. They renamed the carol "The Song From Heaven" and sang it wherever they went.

On Christmas Eve 1832, they were invited to introduce it in the Royal Saxon Court Chapel in Pleissenburg Castle for the King and Queen of Saxony. The Director General of Music, Mr. Pohlenz, had heard the children singing at one of the great fairs in Leipzig where their parents went every year to sell their famous gloves. The unusual music had created an immediate sensation, and word spread rapidly that "the four Strasser children sing like nightingales." It was at his request that the four were invited to sing for the Royal family at this special Christmas Eve celebration. Shortly thereafter, "Silent Night" took its rightful place among the most beautiful Christmas carols in the Christian world, and the passing of time has only added to its luster.

"Silent Night" is one of the most beautiful Christmastime hymns ever written, and it is also a demonstration of how God uses simple events, such as a broken musical instrument, to bless his people with a beautiful song of celebration and praise for the birth of our Lord.

From Starry Heav'n Descending

From starry heav'n descending,
The King of worth untold
Was born in manger dwelling,
Amid the winter's cold.

Infant Savior, Child Divine!
Thy trembling, baby from I see.
O blessed Lord of all!
How great the cost to Thee to show Thy love for me,
How great the cost to Thee to show Thy love for me.

For Thee, the world's creator,
My God, so great, so good!
There was no warning shelter,
Nor wealth of robe, nor food.

Dearest Babe, how poor Thy state,
To lie among the sheep and kine.
O Thou, my Chosen One,
Whatever love is mine, shall more and more be Thine,
Whatever love is mine, shall more and more be Thine.

Thou weepest, Lord, full knowing
Of my ingratitude,
When love alone Thou gavest
And ever sought my good.

Holy Babe, my heart's desire!
I've lived too long away from Thee.
I will no more Thee grieve;
For now my aim shall be to love and honor Thee,
For now my aim shall be to love and honor Thee.

—J. R. Newell

Before we had any idea how much we needed Jesus Christ, God the Father sent him from heaven to live on the earth as a human and to later die for us. God's love for us is so deep and so profound that he sent his Son even before we had any way of expressing our gratitude for that gift.

NATIVITY TWO

The Word Became Flesh

God with Us

Adapted from a sermon by Edward Bouverie Pusey (1800–1882)

"The virgin will be with child and will give birth to a son,
and they will call him Immanuel"—which means,
"God with us."

MATTHEW 1:23

It is part of the majesty of Holy Scripture, as being the word spoken by the Eternal Word, that it is full of manifold meanings, embracing, in itself, all time, and itself, as the Word from Whom it issues, enduring forever, reaching to the height of Heaven and the depths of Hell, God's Holiness and man's sin. It is verified again and again in the endless changes and variations of man's history. Like Him, it speaketh to our hearts, readeth our thoughts long before, scanning us from head to foot, laying us bare to ourselves, piercing or healing us, "a discerner of the intents of the heart." It telleth, in the past, of the future, and the future, as it shall again and again be, till the end come, as being a part of the Omniscience of God. And for this, it needs not, as we, many words. Rather, in few words, it reveals much; herein showing itself different from man's words, in which it comes to us clothed; for we, with many words, scarcely utter all our meaning; it, by reason of the Wisdom and Spirit dwelling in it, declares much in few. And so, when we know one meaning of any words of Holy Scripture, we should beware of thinking that we know all their meanings; lest we cease to search, and seeking not, find not.

Of this sort eminently are those amazing words *God with us.* They contain in themselves the whole history, and course, and means of man's redemption. In their highest sense they express that unfathomable Mystery, that "God" hath been "with us," in our nature, that the Creator has taken His creature into Himself; but, by virtue of that gracious mystery, they declare God's Presence in His Church, and "with" and within the souls of her members.

For all man's history turns on this, to be with or without God, having or not having God with us. All the history of man's decay is but one manifold exhibition of being without God. All his pursuits, arts, inventions, ambition, aggrandisements, passions, lusts, wars, amusements, are, in themselves, but varied forms of godlessness. All his restoration, through revelations, guidances, Providence, chastenings, mercies, is but a course wherein God draweth nigh to him, and draweth him nigh unto Himself. To "live without God in the world," is man's one, though varied misery; "God with us" is the center and circumference of the Divine Mercy.

And of this central mercy, the very center is (how should it not be?) the mystery of this blessed Festival, the Incarnation of the Eternal Word, "God manifest in the flesh." "He Who gave His Son for us, how should He not with Him freely give us all things?" The life of man, as it is the reward of the Saints, is the Sight and Presence of God. All man's fall has been a forgetfulness, a hiding himself from God. As fallen, he could not bear to see God; he could not bear to look upon himself in the Light of God. "The ungodly perish at the Presence of God." Restlessness, busy schemes, ambition, luxury, gluttony, worldliness, study of man's praise, self-deceit, are but man's conscious or unconscious contrivances, to cast a mist about him, so that the glorious light of God should not break in upon him, and shine upon his darkness, and show him how foul is that darkness. All are but varied tokens of one deep disease. And God's remedy has been to accustom men to receive Him. Visibly or invisibly He has come to them, in the garden, ere they were yet cast out: to the Patriarchs, the Prophets, Judges, in the form as though of man: Enoch walked with Him, Unseen, as far as we know, by his bodily eyes; to Noah He came, and taught him to build the ark; to Abraham He promised Himself, as his Reward, and bade him "walk before Me, and be thou perfect;" He deigned to eat and drink with him; to Jacob He gave strength to wrestle with Him, and prevail; to Moses He spake face to face; to Isaiah He showed His glory; to the Prophets He, the Word of God, came; to Job in the whirlwind; to Elijah in the "still small voice;" on Ezekiel His Hand rested; on the Judges He came vehemently down, and bore them on to prevail against His enemies; on the Seventy with Moses, that they prophesied; with the whole people He was, in the pillar of the cloud, in the lightnings of Sinai; "the Face of God,"—i.e., the Son, Who is the Eternal Image of the Eternal Father, went with them, and saved them; He dwelt in the Shechinah, the bright Presence of God, in the Tabernacle and the Temple; with the Three Children He was in a "form as of the Son of God;" to Daniel He appeared "in night visions," as "the Son of Man."

And then, at last, He, Who had thus "not left Himself

without witness," and had been accustoming man to receive Him, came. Before, He had appeared chiefly to the faithful, to be by them acknowledged and adored; now, He came into the world, to be by them rejected. Before, He came as God, for a season, and then withdrawing Himself; now, as Man, to sojourn: before, in glory visible mostly to the bodily eye; now, invisible, except to the eye of faith: before, in Majesty; now, in Humility.

He Who had, from time to time, visited Patriarchs and Prophets, in the *form* of man, came as Man; He Who had shone in visible glory, in the Tabernacle, Himself tabernacled among us, and they whose eyes God opened "beheld His Glory, the Glory as of the Only Begotten of the Father," "God with us." In neither part was He wanting. Perfect God, He became Perfect Man, that He might thereby perfect the whole of man. He "sanctified Himself," that we might be sanctified in Him. He held back from nothing. The Lord of Heaven and earth did not disdain to lie hid in the Virgin's womb; the Omniscient deigned, as Man, to seem to receive and to put forth increase of knowledge; the Eternal Word not "to know to cry, my father, my mother;" He "Who upholdeth all things by the word of His Power" to be carried in the arm; the Eternal Will of the Father not to do His Own Will; the Holy One of God to be tempted by His unholy creature; the Lord of Life to suffer death; the Judge to be judged.

On Christmas Day, we celebrate the Nativity of our Lord Jesus Christ, who revealed God to Jew and Gentile alike—up close and personal. Jesus was and is the same God who visited his people, the Israelites—the fathers, the prophets, and the others—but when he was born of a virgin, he did it in the flesh.

Inspired by What He Saw

"Do not be afraid. I bring you good news of great joy that will be for all the people."

LUKE 2:10

Phillips Brooks (1835–1893) was an influential Episcopalian minister who was born, raised, and educated in Boston, Massachusetts. After graduating from Harvard in 1855, Brooks served as a teacher but found the profession less than fulfilling. After resigning his position as a teacher, he left Boston for Virginia, where he readied himself for ministry at Alexandria Seminary. In 1860, he was ordained, and two years later he was named rector of the Church of the Holy Trinity in Philadelphia, where he became a well-loved and respected minister.

It was in 1865—during his time in Philadelphia—that Brooks took a one-year leave of absence, which he used to tour Europe and the Holy Land. During the week of Christmas, Brooks visited Jerusalem. On Christmas Eve he traveled on horseback from Jerusalem to Bethlehem. That night, he attended a traditional Christmas Eve service at the Church of the Nativity. It was a five-hour service that made a big impression on the thirty-year-old preacher. It was during this visit to the City of David that he saw the site traditionally believed to be where a group of shepherds received the angelic announcement of the birth of Jesus Christ.

This experience moved Brooks deeply, and some three years after he returned home, he wrote the lyrics for one of our most beloved Christmas carols, "O Little Town of Bethlehem":

O little town of Bethlehem,
How still we see thee lie!
Above thy deep and dreamless sleep
The silent stars go by.
Yet in thy dark streets shineth
The everlasting light;
The hopes and fears of all the years
Are met in thee tonight.

For Christ is born of Mary,
And gathered all above,
While mortals sleep, the angels keep
Their watch of wond'ring love.
O morning stars, together
Proclaim the holy birth!
And praises sing to God the King,
And peace to men on earth.

How silently, how silently
The wondrous gift is giv'n!
So God imparts to human hearts
The blessings of His heav'n.
No ear may hear His coming,

But in this world of sin,
Where meek souls will receive Him still,
The dear Christ enters in.

O holy Child of Bethlehem!
Descend to us, we pray;
Cast out our sin and enter in;
Be born in us today.
We hear the Christmas angels
The great glad tidings tell;
O come to us, abide with us,
Our Lord Emmanuel.

Seeing the Holy Land, and specifically the place of Jesus' birth, would be an inspiration to just about any believer. Even more inspiring to each of us, however, should be "seeing" and knowing Jesus Christ, who was born in Bethlehem of Judea.

The Nativity: When the Word Became Flesh

Adapted from a sermon by Saint John of Kronstadt (1829–1908)

The Word became flesh and made his dwelling among us.
We have seen his glory, the glory of the One and Only,
who came from the Father, full of grace and truth.

JOHN 1:14

The Word became flesh; that is, the Son of God, coeternal with God the Father and with the Holy Spirit, became human—having become incarnate of the Holy Spirit and the Virgin Mary. O, wondrous, awesome and saving mystery! The One Who has no beginning took on a beginning according to humanity; the One without flesh assumed flesh. God became man—without ceasing to be God. The Unapproachable One became approachable to all, in the form of a servant.

Why, for what reason was there such a condescension shown on the part of the Creator toward His transgressing creatures—toward humanity which, through an act of its own will had fallen away from God, its Creator?

It was by reason of a supreme, inexpressible mercy toward His creation on the part of the Master, Who could not bear to see the entire race of mankind (which He, in creating, had endowed with such wondrous gifts) enslaved by the devil and thus destined for eternal suffering and torment.

And the Word became flesh! In order to make us earthly beings into heavenly ones. In order to make sinners into saints. In order to raise us up from corruption into incorruption, from earth to heaven; from enslavement to sin and the devil, into the glorious freedom of children of God; from death, into immortality, in order to make us sons of God and to seat us together with Him upon the Throne as His royal children.

O, the boundless compassion of God! O, the inexpressible wisdom of God! O, the great wonder, astounding not only the human mind, but the angelic as well!

Let us glorify God! With the coming of the Son of God in the flesh upon the earth, with His offering Himself up as the sacrifice for our sinful human race, there is given to those who believe the blessing of the Heavenly Father, replacing that curse which had been uttered by God in the beginning.

They are adopted and receive the promise of an eternal inheritance of life.

To humanity orphaned by reason of sin, the Heavenly Father returns anew to Himself through the mystery of rebirth, that is, through baptism and repentance. People are freed of the tormenting, death-bearing authority of the devil, of the afflictions of sin and of various passions. Human nature is deified for the sake of the boundless compassion of the Son of God; and its sins are purified. The defiled are sanctified; the ailing are healed.

Upon those in dishonor are bestowed boundless honor and glory. Those in darkness are enlightened by the Divine light of grace and reason. The human mind is given the rational power of God—we have the mind of Christ (see 1 Corinthians 2:16) says the Holy Apostle Paul. To the human heart, the heart of Christ is given. The perishable is made immortal. Those naked and wounded by sin and by passions are adorned in Divine glory. Those who hunger and thirst are filled by the nourishing and soul-strengthening Word of God and by the most pure Body and Divine Blood of Christ. The inconsolable are consoled. Those ravaged by the devil have been, and continue to be, delivered by God.

What, then, dear brethren, is required of us in order that we might avail ourselves of the grace brought unto us from on high by the coming to earth of the Son of God?

What is necessary, first of all, is faith in the Son of God; in the Gospel as the salvation-bestowing heavenly teaching; a true repentance of sins and the correction of life and of heart; communion in prayer and in the holy mysteries; the knowledge and fulfillment of Christ's commandments. Also necessary are the virtues: Christian humility, almsgiving, continence, purity and chastity, simplicity and goodness of heart.

Let us, then, O brother and sister, bring these virtues as a gift to the One Who was born for the sake of our salvation—let us bring them in place of the gold, frankincense, and myrrh which the Magi brought Him, as to One Who is King, God, and Man, come to die for us. This, from us, shall be the most-pleasing form of sacrifice to God and to the Infant Jesus Christ.

The Gospel of John doesn't say anything directly about the birth of Jesus, but it tells us the significance of that event: "The Word

became flesh and made his dwelling among us." That means that God himself put on the flesh of a human being so that he could be the Savior he knew we needed.

God with Us!

From Morning and Evening *by Charles H. Spurgeon (1834–1892)*

"The virgin will be with child and will give birth to a son, and will call him Immanuel."

ISAIAH 7:14

Let us today go down to Bethlehem, and in company with wondering shepherds and adoring Magi, let us see him who was born King of the Jews, for we by faith can claim an interest in him, and can sing, "*Unto us* a child is born, *unto us* a son is given." Jesus is Jehovah incarnate, our Lord and our God, and yet our brother and friend; let us adore and admire. Let us notice at the very first glance *his miraculous conception*. It was a thing unheard of before, and unparalleled since, that a virgin should conceive and bear a Son.

The first promise ran thus, "*The seed of the woman,*" not the offspring of the man. Since venturous woman led the way in the sin which brought forth Paradise lost, she, and she alone, ushers in the Regainer of Paradise. Our Savior, although truly man, was as to his human nature the Holy One of God. Let us reverently bow before the holy Child whose innocence restores to manhood its ancient glory; and let us pray that he may be formed in us, the hope of glory.

Fail not to note *his humble parentage*. His mother has been described simply as "a virgin," not a princess, or prophetess, nor a matron of large estate. True the blood of kings ran in her veins; nor was her mind a weak and untaught one, for she could sing most sweetly a song of praise; but yet how humble her position, how poor the man to whom she stood affianced, and how miserable the accommodation afforded to the new-born King!

Immanuel, God with us in our nature, in our sorrow, in our lifework, in our punishment, in our grave, and now with us, or rather we with him, in resurrection, ascension, triumph, and Second Advent splendor.

The apostle Matthew understood what was happening when Jesus was born in Bethlehem. He knew that it was a fulfillment of the promises made long ago that God himself would be born in Bethlehem. That is why he added this definition of the name Immanuel: "God with us" (Matthew 1:23).

The Wonder of Christ's Nativity

Adapted from the writings of Gregory of Neocaesarea (213–270)

On the present great day He is born of the Virgin, having overcome the natural order of things. He is higher than wedlock and free from defilement. It sufficed that He the preceptor of purity should shine forth gloriously, to emerge from a pure and undefiled womb. For He is that Same, Who in the beginning did create Adam from the virgin soil, and from Adam without wedlock did bring forth for him his wife Eve.

And as Adam was without wife before that he had a wife, and the first woman then was brought into the world, so likewise on the present day the Virgin without man gives birth to that One, about Whom spoke the prophet: "He—is Man, who is he that doth know Him?" The Man Christ, clearly seen by mankind, born of God, is such that womankind was needed to perfect that of mankind, so that perfectly would be born man for woman.

And just as from Adam was taken woman, without impairment and without diminishing of his masculine nature, so also from woman without man was needed to bring forth a man, similar to the bringing forth of Eve, so that Adam be not extolled in that without his means woman should bring forth woman. Therefore the Virgin without cohabitation with man gave birth to God the Word, made Man, so that in equal measure it was by the same miracle to bestow equal honor to both the one and the other half—man and woman.

And just as from Adam was taken woman without his diminishing, so likewise from the Virgin was taken the body (Born of Her), wherein also the Virgin did not undergo diminishing, and Her virginity did not suffer harm. Adam dwelt well and unharmed, when the rib was taken from him: and so without defilement dwelt the Virgin, when from Her was brought forth God the Word. For this sort of reason particularly the word assumed of the Virgin Her flesh and Her bodily garb, so that He be not accounted innocent of the sin of Adam. Since man stung by sin had become a vessel and instrument of evil, Christ took upon Himself this receptacle of sin into His Own flesh so that, the Creator having been co-united with the body, it should thus be freed from the foulness of the enemy, and man thus be clothed in an eternal body, which be neither perished nor destroyed for all eternity.

Moreover, He that is become the God-Man is born, not as ordinarily man is born—He is born as God made Man, manifest of this by His Own Divine power, since if He were born according to the general laws of nature, the Word would seem something imperfect. Therefore, He was born of the Virgin and shone forth; therefore, having been born, He preserved unharmed the virginal womb, so that the hitherto unheard of manner of the Nativity should be for us a sign of great mystery.

Is Christ God? Christ is God by nature, but not by

the order of nature did He become Man. Thus we declare and in truth believe, calling to witness the seal of intact virginity: as Almighty Creator of the womb and virginity, He chose an unshameful manner of birth and was made Man, as He did will.

On this great day, now being celebrated, God hath appeared as Man, as Pastor of the nation of Israel, Who hath enlivened all the universe with His goodness. O dear warriors, glorious champions for mankind, who did preach Bethlehem as a place of Theophany and the Nativity of the Son of God, who have made known to all the world the Lord of all, lying in a manger, and did point out God contained within a narrow cave!

We should focus and meditate on the wonder of that day when God became man, when he put on human flesh and started a life among us. We should take time to focus on the wonder of that event year-round but especially as we celebrate and enjoy the Christmas season.

A Christmas Carol

The shepherds went their hasty way,
And found the lowly stable-shed
Where the Virgin-Mother lay:
And now they checked their eager tread,
For to the Babe, that at her bosom clung,
A Mother's song the Virgin-Mother sung.

They told her how a glorious light,
Streaming from a heavenly throng.
Around them shone, suspending night!
While sweeter than a mother's song,
Blest Angels heralded the Savior's birth,
Glory to God on high! and Peace on Earth.

She listened to the tale divine,
And closer still the Babe she pressed:
And while she cried, the Babe is mine!
The milk rushed faster to her breast:
Joy rose within her, like a summer's morn;
Peace, Peace on Earth! the Prince of Peace is born.

Thou Mother of the Prince of Peace,
Poor, simple, and of low estate!

That strife should vanish, battle cease,
O why should this thy soul elate?
Sweet Music's loudest note, the Poet's story,
Didst thou ne'er love to hear of fame and glory?

And is not War a youthful king,
A stately Hero clad in mail?
Beneath his footsteps laurels spring;
Him Earth's majestic monarchs hail
Their friends, their playmate! and his bold bright eye
Compels the maiden's love-confessing sigh.

Tell this in some more courtly scene,
To maids and youths in robes of state!
I am a woman poor and mean,
And wherefore is my soul elate.
War is a ruffian, all with guilt defiled,
That from the aged father's tears his child!

A murderous fiend, by fiends adored,
He kills the sire and starves the son;
The husband kills, and from her board
Steals all his widow's toil had won;
Plunders God's world of beauty; rends away
All safety from the night, all comfort from the day.

Then wisely is my soul elate,
That strife should vanish, battle cease:
I'm poor and of low estate,
The Mother of the Prince of Peace.

Joy rises in me, like a summer's morn:
Peace, Peace on Earth! The Prince of Peace is born!

—Samuel Taylor Coleridge (1772–1834)

The story of the birth of Jesus Christ was one of many twists and turns, all of which were divinely orchestrated. Everything that took place at that pivotal time in history was for one reason: so that the Prince of Peace could be born!

The Light of the World

Adapted from the writings of Evelyn Underhill (1875–1941)

When we come to the first window at the east end of the aisle, the morning light comes through it. It is the window of the Incarnation. It brings us at once to the mingled homeliness and mystery of the Christian revelation and of our own little lives. It is full of family pictures and ideas—the birth of Christ, the Shepherds and the Magi, the little boy of Nazareth, the wonderful experience in the Temple, the long quiet years in the carpenter's shop. There seems nothing so very supernatural about the first stage. But stand back and look—Mira! Mira!

We are being shown here something profoundly significant about human life—"God speaks in a Son," a baby son, and reverses all our pet values. He speaks in our language and shows us his secret beauty on our scale. We have got to begin not by an arrogant other-worldliness, but by a humble recognition that human things can be holy, very full of God, and that high-minded speculations about his nature need not be holy at all; that all life is engulfed in him and he can reach out to us anywhere at any level.

As the Christmas Day gospel takes us back to the mystery of the divine nature—In the beginning was the Word—so let us begin by thinking of what Saint Catherine called the "Ocean Pacific of the Godhead" enveloping all life. The depth and richness of his being are entirely unknown to us, poor little scraps as we are! And yet the unlimited life who is Love right through—who loves and is wholly present where he loves, on every plane and at every point—so loved the world as to desire to give his essential thought, the deepest secrets of his heart to this small, fugitive, imperfect creation—to us. That seems immense.

And then the heavens open and what is disclosed? A baby, God manifest in the flesh. The stable, the manger, the straw; poverty, cold, darkness—these form the setting of the divine gift. In this child God gives his supreme message to the soul—Spirit to spirit—but in a human way. Outside in the fields the heavens open and the shepherds look up astonished to find the music and radiance of reality all around them. But inside, our closest contact with that same reality is being offered to us in the very simplest, homeliest way—emerging right into our ordinary life. A baby—just that. We are not told that the blessed, virgin Mary saw the angels or heard the Gloria in the air. Her initiation had been quite different, like the quiet voice speaking in our deepest prayer—"The Lord is with thee!" "Behold the handmaid of the Lord." Humble self-abandonment is quite enough to give us God.

Think of the tremendous contrast, transcendent and homely, brought together here as a clue to the Incarnation—the hard life of the poor, the absolute surrender and helplessness of babyhood and the unmeasured outpouring of divine life.

The Christmas mystery has two parts: the Nativity and the epiphany. A deep instinct made the Church separate these two feasts. In the first we commemorate God's humble entrance into human life, the emergence and birth of the holy, and in the second its manifestation to the world, the revelation of the supernatural made in that life. And the two phases concern our inner lives very closely too. The first only happens in order that the second may happen, and the second cannot happen without the first. Christ is a Light to lighten the Gentiles as well as the glory of his people Israel. Think of what the Gentile was when these words were written—an absolute outsider. All cozy religious exclusiveness falls before that thought. The Light of the world is not the sanctuary lamp in your favorite church.

It is easy for the devout to join up with the shepherds and fall into place at the crib and look out into the surrounding night and say, "Look at those extraordinary intellectuals wandering about after a star, with no religious sense at all! Look at that clumsy camel, what an unspiritual animal it is! We know the ox and the ass are the right animals to have! Look what queer gifts and odd types of self-consecration they are bringing; not the sort of people who come to church!" But remember that the child who began by receiving these very unexpected pilgrims had a woman of the streets for his faithful friend and two thieves for his comrades at the end: and looking at these two extremes let us try to learn a little of the height and breadth and depth of his love—and then apply it to our own lives.

Beholding his glory is only half our job. In our souls too the mysteries must be brought forth; we are not really Christians till that has been done. "The Eternal Birth," says Eckhart, "must take place in you." And another mystic says human nature is like a stable inhabited by the ox of passion and the ass of prejudice; animals which take up a lot of room and which I suppose most of us are feeding on the quiet. And it is there between them, pushing them out, that Christ must be born and in their very manger he must be laid—and they will be the first to fall on their knees before him. Sometimes Christians seem far nearer to those animals than to Christ in his simple poverty, self-abandoned to God.

The birth of Christ in our souls is for a purpose beyond ourselves: it is because his manifestation in the world must be through us. Every Christian is, as it were, part of the dust-laden air which shall radiate the glowing epiphany of God, catch and reflect his golden Light. Ye are the light of the world—but only because you are enkindled, made radiant by the one Light of the world. And being kindled, we have got to get on with it, be useful. As Christ said in one of his ironical flashes, "Do not light a candle in order to stick it under the bed!" Some people make a virtue of religious skulking.

When you don't see any startling marks of your own religious condition or your usefulness to God, think of the baby in the stable and the little Boy in the streets of Nazareth. The very life was there which was to change the whole history of the human race. There was not much to show for it. But there is entire continuity between the stable and the Easter garden and the thread that unites them is the will of God. The childlike simple prayer of Nazareth was the right preparation for the awful privilege of the Cross.

Just so the light of the Spirit is to unfold gently and steadily within us, till at last our final stature, all God designed for us, is attained. It is an organic process, a continuous divine action, not a series of jerks. So on the one hand there should be no strain, impatience, self-willed effort in our prayer and self-discipline; and on the other, no settling down. A great flexibility, a gentle acceptance of what comes to us and a still gentler acceptance of the fact that much we see in others is still out of our reach. We must keep our prayer free, youthful—full of confidence and full of initiative too.

The mystics keep telling us that the goal of that prayer and the goal of that hidden life which should itself become more and more of a prayer, is "union with God." We use that phrase often, much too often to preserve the wholesome sense of its awe-fullness. For what does union with God mean? It is not a nice feeling we get in devout moments. That may or may not be a by-product of union—probably not. It can never be its substance.

Union with God means every bit of our human nature transfigured in Christ, woven up into his creative life and activity, absorbed into his redeeming purpose, heart, soul, mind and strength. Each time it happens it means that one of God's creatures has achieved its destiny.

Jesus' birth was for the purpose of bringing his light to each of us as individuals, and it's a light he intended for us to shine to the world around us—just because we know him and fellowship with him personally.

Born to Save!

Adapted from the writings of Athanasius the Great (298–373)

"He will save his people from their sins."

MATTHEW 1:21

What was God to do in face of the dehumanizing of mankind, this universal hiding of the knowledge of himself through the wiles of the evil one? What was he to do in answer to the fall of man into sin and corruption?

Was he to remain silent before so great a wrong and let men go on being thus deceived and kept in ignorance of himself? If so, what was the use of having made them in his own image in the first place? It would surely have been better for them always to have been brutes, rather than to revert to that condition when once they had shared the nature of the Word. Again, things being as they were, what was the use of their ever having had the knowledge of God? Surely it would have been better for God never to have bestowed it, than that men should subsequently be found unworthy to receive it.

Similarly, what possible profit could it be to God himself, who made men, if when made they did not worship him, but regarded others as their makers? This would be tantamount to his having made them for others and not for himself. Even an earthly king, though he is only a man, does not allow lands that he has colonized to pass into other hands or to desert to other rulers, but sends letters and friends and even visits them himself to recall them to their allegiance, rather than allow his work to be undone. How much more, then, will God be patient and painstaking with his creatures, that they be not led astray from him to the service of those that are not, and that all the more because such error means for them sheer ruin, and because it is not right that those who had once shared his image should be destroyed.

What, then, was God to do? What else could he possibly do, being God, but renew his image in mankind, so that through it men might once more come to know him? But how? How could this be done save by the coming of the very image himself, our Savior Jesus Christ? Men could not have done it, for they are only *made after* the image; nor could angels have done it, for they are not the images of God at all.

The Word of God came in his own person, because it was he alone, the image of the Father who could recreate man made after the image.

In order to effect this re-creation, however, he had first to do away with death and corruption. Therefore he assumed a human body, in order that in it death might once for all be destroyed, and that men might be renewed according to the image. He assumed that human body when he was born in Bethlehem two thousand years ago, lived as a human being, and then died a sacrificial death for all of humankind.

Jesus didn't come to earth to be born of a virgin and laid in a manger just so believers could have a yearly celebration. His purpose was much more important and profound than that. As Jesus himself said, "The Son of Man came to seek and to save what was lost" (Luke 19:10).

Some Christmas Poetry

Christmas 1

After all pleasures as I rid one day,
My horse and I, both tired, body and mind,
With full cry of affections, quite astray;
I took up the next inn I could find.

There when I came, whom found I but my dear,
My dearest Lord, expecting till the grief
Of pleasures brought me to Him, ready there
To be all passengers' most sweet relief?

Oh Thou, whose glorious, yet contracted light,
Wrapt in night's mantle, stole into a manger;
Since my dark soul and brutish is Thy right,
To man of all beasts be not Thou a stranger:

Furnish and deck my soul, that Thou mayst have
A better lodging, than a rack, or grave.

Christmas 2

The shepherds sing; and shall I silent be?
My God, no hymn for Thee?
My soul's a shepherd too; a flock it feeds
Of thoughts, and words, and deeds.

The pasture is Thy word: the streams, Thy grace
Enriching all the place.
Shepherd and flock shall sing, and all my powers
Outsing the daylight hours.
Then will we chide the sun for letting night
Take up his place and right:
We sing one common Lord; wherefore he should
Himself the candle hold.
I will go searching, till I find a sun
Shall stay, till we have done;
A willing shiner, that shall shine as gladly,
As frost-nipped suns look sadly.
Then will we sing, and shine all our own day,
And one another pay:
His beams shall cheer my breast, and both so twine,
Till ev'n His beams sing, and my music shine.

—George Herbert (1593–1633)

The Birthday of Life

Adapted from a sermon by Leo the Great (fifth century)

"Today in the town of David a Savior has been born to you; he is Christ the Lord."

LUKE 2:11

Dearly beloved, today our Savior is born; let us rejoice. Sadness should have no place on the birthday of life. The fear of death has been swallowed up; life brings us joy with the promise of eternal happiness.

No one is shut out from this joy; all share the same reason for rejoicing. Our Lord, victor over sin and death, finding no man free from sin, came to free us all. Let the saint rejoice as he sees the palm of victory at hand. Let the sinner be glad as he receives the offer of forgiveness. Let the pagan take courage as he is summoned to life.

In the fullness of time, chosen in the unfathomable depths of God's wisdom, the Son of God took for himself our common humanity in order to reconcile it with its Creator. He came to overthrow the devil, the origin of death, in that very nature by which he had overthrown mankind.

And so at the birth of our Lord the angels sing in joy:

Glory to God in the highest, and they proclaim peace to men of good will as they see the heavenly Jerusalem being built from all the nations of the world. When the angels on high are so exultant at this marvelous work of God's goodness, what joy should it not bring to the lowly hearts of men?

Beloved, let us give thanks to God the Father, through his Son, in the Holy Spirit, because in his great love for us he took pity on us, and when we were dead in our sins he brought us to life with Christ, so that in him we might be a new creation. Let us throw off our old nature and all its ways and, as we have come to birth in Christ, let us renounce the works of the flesh.

Christian, remember your dignity, and now that you share in God's own nature, do not return by sin to your former base condition. Bear in mind who is your head and of whose body you are a member. Do not forget that you have been rescued from the power of darkness and brought into the light of God's Kingdom.

Through the sacrament of baptism you have become a temple of the Holy Spirit. Do not drive away so great a guest by evil conduct and become again a slave to the devil, for your liberty was bought by the blood of Christ.

Christmas, the day we celebrate the birth of Christ, is a day when we can celebrate freedom from what we once were and freedom to be what God made us to be in the first place. It is a day to celebrate Christ's physical birth and our new spiritual birth.

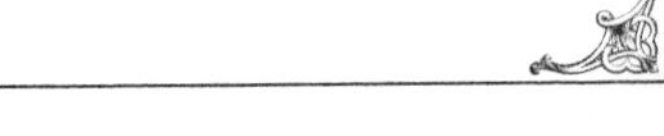

NATIVITY THREE

Christ Our Substitute

On the Night of Nativity

Adapted from the writings of Ephraim the Syrian (306–373)

Pure is the present night, in which the Pure One appeared, who came to purify us! Let our hearing be pure, and the sight of our eyes chaste, and the feeling of the heart holy, and the speech of the mouth sincere!

The present night is the night of reconciliation; therefore, let no one be wroth against his brother and offend him!

This night gave peace to the whole world, and so, let no one threaten. This is the night of the Most Meek One; let no one be cruel!

This is the night of the Humble One; let no one be proud!

Now is the day of joy; let us not take revenge for offences! Now is the day of good will; let us not be harsh. On this day of tranquility, let us not become agitated by anger!

Today God came unto sinners; let not the righteous exalt himself over sinners!

Today the Most Rich One became poor for our sake; let the rich man invite the poor to his table!

Today we received a gift which we did not ask for; let us bestow alms to those who cry out to us and beg!

The present day has opened the door of heaven to our prayers; let us also open our door to those who ask of us forgiveness!

Today the Godhead placed upon Himself the seal of humanity, and humanity has been adorned with the seal of the Godhead!

Now the day of mercy has shown forth! Let no one persecute his neighbor with revenge for the wrong he has caused him! The day of joy has arrived! Let no one be guilty of causing sorrow and grief to another person. This is a cloudless and bright day!

Let anger be stilled for it disturbs peace and tranquility. This is the day in which God descended to sinners! Let the righteous man be ashamed to exalt himself over sinners.

This is the day when the Lord of creation came to servants! Let the master of the house humble himself in similar love to his servants. This is the day on which the Wealthy One became poor for our sake! Let not the rich be ashamed to share their table with the poor.

Jesus had spent all of eternity in perfect fellowship with the heavenly Father. But he humbled himself and gave up everything in order to come to earth to be the perfect example, the perfect teacher, the perfect healer, the perfect Savior. It is because of his sacrifice that we can join with the angels in heaven, singing, "Glory to God in the highest!"

Carol

I sing the birth was born tonight,
The author both of life and light;
The angels so did sound it,
And like the ravished shepherds said,
Who saw the light, and were afraid,
Yet searched, and true they found it.

The Son of God, the eternal king,
That did us all salvation bring,
And freed our soul from danger,
He whom the whole world could not take,
The Word, which heaven and earth did make,
Was now laid in a manger.

The Father's wisdom will it so,
The Son's obedience knew no No;
Both wills were in one stature,
And, as that wisdom had decreed,
The Word was now made flesh indeed,
And took on him our nature.

What comfort by him we do win,
Whom make himself the price of sin,

To make us heirs of glory!
To see this babe, all innocence,
A martyr born in our defence,
Can man forget the story?

—BEN JONSON (1572–1637)

The Nativity is a story none of us who believe in Jesus Christ should ever forget. It was the moment when Jesus started a life of absolute obedience to the Father, which would culminate in his being our sacrifice for sin before a holy God.

True Way of Keeping Christmas

Excerpted and adapted from a sermon by George Whitefield (1714–1770)

"She will give birth to a son, and you are to give him the name Jesus, because he will save his people from their sins."

MATTHEW 1:21

When we consider the condescension and love of the Lord Jesus Christ, in submitting to be born of a virgin, herself a poor sinful creature, we can do nothing but celebrate. That is especially true when we consider that he knew how he would be treated in this world—that he was to be despised, scoffed at, and at last to die a painful, shameful, humiliating death. He knew that he would be treated as the dregs of all humankind, that he would be used, not like the son of man, and, therefore, not at all like the Son of God.

When we think of these things, we will even more appreciate the love of the Lord Jesus Christ, who was so willing to offer himself as a ransom for the sins of the people, who, when the fullness of time was come, came to earth, made of a woman, made under the law: he came according to the eternal counsel of the Father. Jesus came, not in glory or in splendor, not like him who brought all salvation with him, but he came, born in a stable and laid in a manger; where oxen were his companions.

O amazing condescension of the Lord Jesus Christ, who stooped to such low and poor things for our sake. What love is this, what great and wonderful love was here, that the Son of God should come into our world in so mean a condition, to deliver us from the sin and misery in which we were involved by our fall in our first parents!

If we but consider into what state and how far from God we are fallen and how vile our natures were . . . and how incapable we are of restoring ourselves that image of God to our souls . . . and that the Lord Jesus Christ came to restore us to that favor with God . . . that Jesus Christ not only came down with an intent to do it, but actually accomplished all that was in his heart towards us . . . that we might find kindness and mercy in God's sight—surely this calls for some return of thanks on our part to our dear Redeemer.

Shall we not remember the birth of our Jesus? Shall we yearly celebrate the birth of our earthly king while forgetting the birth of the King of kings? God forbid!

My dear brethren, let us celebrate and keep this festival of our church, with joy in our hearts. Let the birth of a Redeemer, who redeemed us from sin, from wrath, from death, from hell, be always remembered. May this Savior's love never be forgotten!

May we sing forth all his love and glory as long as life shall last here, and through an endless eternity in the world above! May we chant forth the wonders of redeeming love, and the riches of free grace, amidst angels and archangels, cherubim and seraphim, without intermission, forever and ever!

It is only right that we should celebrate and commemorate the birth of our Savior, who came to earth not to benefit himself but to give everything he had to a humanity so lost that it could never have found its way back to God. As we celebrate and commemorate his birth, let us keep who he is and what he has done for us at the center of everything we do.

The Completeness of the Substitution

Adapted from writings of Horatius Bonar (1808–1889)

In person and in work, in life and in death, Jesus Christ is the sinner's Substitute. His vicariousness is co-extensive with the sins and wants of those whom he represents, and covers all the different periods as well as the varied circumstances of their lives.

Jesus entered our world as the Substitute: "There was no room for [him] in the inn" (Luke 2:7, KJV)—the inn of Bethlehem, the city of David, his own city. "Though he was rich, yet for your sakes he became poor," Paul wrote of him (2 Corinthians 8:9, KJV).

Jesus began his life in poverty and in banishment. He was not to be allowed to be born or to die as anything but an outcast man. "Outside the city" (Hebrews 13:12) was his position as he entered and as he left our earth. Man would not give even a roof to shelter or a cradle to receive the helpless babe. It was as the Substitute that he was the outcast from the first moment of his birth. His vicarious life began in the manger. For what can this poverty mean, this rejection by man, this outcast condition, but that his sin-bearing had begun?

The name, too, that met him as he came into our

world intimated the same truth: "You are to give him the name Jesus, because he will save his people from their sins" (Matthew 1:21). His *name* proclaimed his mission and his work to be salvation; "Jehovah the Savior" (Jesus) is that by which the infant is called. As the *Savior,* he comes forth from the womb; as the *Savior,* he lies in the manger; and if he is the Savior, he is the Substitute. The name *Jesus* was not given to him merely in reference to the cross, but to his whole life below. Therefore did Mary say, "My soul glorifies the Lord and my spirit rejoices in God *my Savior*" (Luke 1:46-47). Therefore also did the angel say to the shepherds, "Today in the town of David *a Savior* has been born to you; he is Christ the Lord" (Luke 2:11).

Scarcely is Jesus born that his blood is shed. Circumcision deals with him as one guilty and needing the sign of cleansing. He knew no sin, yet he is circumcised. He was not born in sin, nor shapen in iniquity, but was "the holy one" (Luke 1:35), yet he is circumcised as other children of Abraham, for "he took on him the seed of Abraham" (Hebrews 2:16, KJV).

Why was he circumcised if not as the Substitute? The rite proclaimed his vicarious birth, as truly as did the cross his vicarious death. "God made him who had no sin to be sin for us, so that in him we might become the righteousness of God" (2 Corinthians 5:21). This was the beginning of that obedience in virtue of which righteousness comes to us; as it is written, "For just as through the disobedience of the one man the many were made sinners, so also through the obedience of the one man the many will be made righteous" (Romans 5:19). For he himself testified concerning his baptism, "it is proper for us to do this to fulfill all righteousness" (Matthew 3:15); and what was true of his baptism was no less true of his circumcision. The pain and the blood and the bruising of his tender body, connected with that symbol of shame, are inexplicable save on the supposition that even in infancy he was the vicarious one, not indeed bearing sin in the full sense and manner in which he bore it on the cross (for without *death*, sin-bearing could not have been consummated), but still bearing it in measure, according to the condition of his years. Even then He was "the Lamb of God."

From the moment he was born, Jesus took on the role of our substitute and representative. That's because he came as our Savior. In his life and in his death, Jesus was and is everything we need in order to be reconciled to the Father—all because he was our substitute.

All for Our Sake

Adapted from ancient Syriac liturgy

Suddenly a great company of the heavenly host appeared with the angel, praising God and saying, "Glory to God in the highest, and on earth peace to men on whom his favor rests."

LUKE 2:13-14

Jesus Christ, radiant center of glory, image of our God, the invisible Father, revealer of his eternal designs, Prince of Peace, Father of the world to come.

For our sake he took the likeness of a slave, becoming flesh in the womb of a virgin, for our sake, wrapped in swaddling bands and laid in a manger adored by the shepherds and hymned by the angelic powers, who sang: Glory to God in the heavens and on earth peace and good will to men.

Make us worthy, Lord, to celebrate and to conclude in peace the feast which magnifies the rising of Thy light, by avoiding empty words, working with justice, fleeing from the passions, and raising up the spirit above earthly goods.

Bless Thy Church, formed long ago to be united with Thou through Thy life-giving blood. Come to the aid of Thy faithful shepherds, of the priests and the teachers of the Gospel.

Bless Thy faithful whose only hope is in Thy mercy; Christian souls, the sick, those who are tormented in spirit, and those who have asked us to pray for them.

Have pity, in Thy infinite clemency, and preserve us in fitness to receive the future, endless, good things. We celebrate Thy glorious Nativity with the Father who sent thee for our redemption, with the life-giving Spirit, now and forever and through all ages. Amen.

As Christians, we understand that Jesus died a sacrificial death for us on the cross. But that isn't all he did for us. Even in submitting himself to come to earth as a baby, Jesus was assuming the role of servant. Everything he did, from the moment of his birth forward, was for the purpose of blessing us.

No Room in the Inn

Adapted from the works of Charles H. Spurgeon (1834–1892)

She gave birth to her firstborn, a son. She wrapped him in cloths and placed him in a manger, because there was no room for them in the inn.

LUKE 2:7

It was necessary that Our Lord Jesus Christ would be born in Bethlehem Ephrathah, which is located in the land of Judah, for this was in accordance to the Word of the Lord which was spoken by His servant Micah, "But you, Bethlehem Ephrathah, though you are small among the clans of Judah, out of you will come for me one who will be ruler over Israel, whose origins are from of old, from ancient times" (Micah 5:2). But how could one bring about public recognition of the ancestry of an obscure carpenter and an unknown maiden? How would the local innkeepers know anything about these two humble persons?

The second part of this story is that Mary lived in Nazareth, in Galilee, and there seemed to be every probability that the birth would take place there. Indeed, the time of her delivery was so near that, unless absolutely compelled, she would not likely undertake such a long and tedious journey to the southern province of Judea. How are these two realities to be harmonized? How do you get this obscure couple living in Nazareth to make the hard journey to Bethlehem when Mary is about to give birth? How do you get the official stamp of the Roman Empire to be affixed to the pedigree of the coming Son of David, and to make Bethlehem the place of the Nativity?

A little tyrant, Herod, in a show of independent spirit, offends the greater tyrant, Augustus, who informs him that he will no longer treat him as a friend, but as a slave. And although Herod makes the most humiliating submission, and his friends at the Roman court intercede for him, yet Augustus, to show his displeasure, orders a census to be taken of all the Jewish people, in order to make preparations for a contemplated taxation, which was not carried out until some ten years later.

Even the winds and the waves are not more fickle than a tyrant's will; but the Ruler of the wind and the waves knows how to rule the perverse spirits of princes. The Lord our God has a bridle for the wildest war horse, and a hook for the most terrible sea monster.

Dictatorial Caesars are but puppets moved with invisible strings, mere slaves to the King of kings. Augustus must become offended with Herod; he is compelled to tax the people; it is imperative that a census be taken; no, it is necessary that inconvenient, harsh, and tyrannical regulations would be published, and every person must return to the town to which he was reputed to belong; thus Mary is brought to Bethlehem, Jesus Christ is born as prophesied. Moreover, He is recognized officially as being descended from David by the fact that his mother came to Bethlehem as being of that lineage, remained there, and returned to Galilee without having her claims questioned, although the jealousy of all the women of the clan would have been aroused had an intruder ventured to claim a place among the few females to whom the birth of the Messiah had been prophesied to occur. Note the wisdom by the God of providence in the way everything here was so well orchestrated.

When all the people of the house of David were thus compelled to go to Bethlehem, the sparse accommodations of the little town were soon exhausted. Doubtless friends and relatives took in their out-of-town guests until their houses were full, but Joseph had no such willing relatives in the town. There was the "caravansary," which was provided in every village, where free accommodations were given to travelers; this too was full, for coming from a distance, and compelled to travel slowly because of Mary's condition, the humble couple arrived late in the day.

The rooms within the great brick square (caravansary) were already occupied with families; there remained no better lodging—even for a woman experiencing birth pains—than one of the crude and rough places appropriate for animals. The stall of the donkey was the only place where the child could be born. By hanging a curtain at its front, and perhaps tying up the animal on the outside to block the passage, the needed seclusion could be obtained, and here, in the stable, was the King of Glory born, and he was laid in the manger.

Now, is there a mystery here in that the Savior is laid where weary animals receive their food? I believe our Lord was laid in the manger where the beasts were fed, to show "that even beast-like men may come to him and live." No creature can be so degraded that Christ cannot lift it up. It may fall, and seem to most certainly fall to hell, but the long and strong arm of Christ can reach it even in its most desperate degradation; he can bring it up from apparently hopeless ruin. If there is one who has strolled in here this morning whom society abhors, and who abhors himself, my Master in the stable with the beasts presents himself as able to save the vilest of the vile, and to accept the worst of the worst even now. Believe in him and he will make you a new creature.

In his sovereignty, God orchestrated a long chain of events to make sure that the world would know that Jesus Christ was the long-awaited Messiah/Savior. And he did that for one reason: so that each and every one of us could be made into new creatures through the work of his only Son.

To You Christ Is Born

Excerpted and adapted from a 1530 Christmas sermon by Martin Luther (1483–1546)

"Today in the town of David a Savior has been born to you; he is Christ the Lord."

LUKE 2:11

We have all heard the story of the birth of the Lord Jesus Christ from the Gospel of Luke. This account tells us how and where Christ was born and how the angel announced the birth of the Lord and Savior to the shepherds who were minding their flocks nearby. It tells us what in human logic is hard to believe: that this infant Jesus, who was God in the flesh, was born of a virgin. Difficult to believe . . . except for those who, through faith, know him as their Lord and Savior.

This is what separates us from unbelievers: Not just knowing that we know that Christ, born of a virgin, is the Lord and Savior, but that Christ, born of a virgin, is *your* Lord and Savior. When you have that personal knowledge, you are able to say in your heart, "I hear the Word that sounds from heaven and says: This child who is born of the virgin is not only his mother's son. I have more than the mother's estate. He is more mine than Mary's, for he was born for me, for the angel said, 'To you' is born the Savior." Then you can and should say, "Amen, I thank you, dear Lord."

It is easier to believe that Christ, born of a virgin, is the Lord and Savior for great people like Peter and Paul, but he wasn't born for a sinner like me. But if that is what you believe, it is not enough—unless you were to add that you have faith that he was born for you.

Those who can sing, "The Son, who is proclaimed to be a Lord and Savior, is my Savior" and can confirm the message of the angel and say "yes" to it and believe it in their hearts have assurance, joy, and confidence before God.

When we can say that we accept the gift the angel announced as our own, knowing that it was meant for us personally, then we can know we have peace with God, and we can feel joy and laughter in our hearts, knowing that sin can do nothing against us: "If God is for us, who can be against us?" (Romans 8:31).

Jesus was born of a virgin so that he could live a perfect life and die a sacrificial death for the sins of the world. But as individuals, we need to take that a step further, personalizing it so that we can say that the Savior was born for us personally.

On the Birthday of Christ

Excerpted and adapted from a sermon by Gregory Nazianzus (Gregory the Theologian, 329–389)

Suddenly a great company of the heavenly host appeared with the angel, praising God and saying, "Glory to God in the highest, and on earth peace to men on whom his favor rests."

LUKE 2:13-14

Christ is born, glorify him! Christ from heaven; go out to meet him! Christ on earth; be exalted! Sing unto the Lord all the whole earth; and that I may join both in one word, let the heavens rejoice, and let the earth be glad, for him who is of heaven and then of earth. Christ in the flesh—rejoice with trembling and with joy; with trembling because of your sins, with joy because of your hope. . . . Who does not worship him who is from the beginning? Who does not glorify him who is the Last?"

Again the darkness is past; again Light is made; again Egypt is punished with darkness; again Israel is enlightened by a pillar. The people that sat in the darkness of ignorance, let it see the Great Light of full knowledge. Old things are passed away, behold all things are become new. The letter gives way, the Spirit comes to the front. The shadows flee away, the Truth comes in upon them. The laws of nature are upset; the world above must be filled.

Christ commands it, let us not set ourselves against him. O clap your hands together all you people, because unto us a Child is born, and a Son given unto us, whose government is upon his shoulder (for with the Cross it is raised up), and his name is called The Angel of the Great Counsel of the Father. Prepare the way of the Lord: I too will cry the power of this day. He who is not carnal is Incarnate; the Son of God becomes the Son of Man, Jesus Christ the same yesterday, and today, and forever.

The Festival is the Theophany, or Birthday, for it is called both—two titles being given to the one thing. For God was manifested to man by birth. On the one hand Being, and eternally Being, of the Eternal Being, above cause and word, for there was not word before The Word; and on the other hand for our sakes also Becoming, that he Who gives us our being might also give us our Well-being, or rather might restore us by his Incarnation, when we had by wickedness fallen from well-being.

This is our present Festival; it is this which we are celebrating, the Coming of God to Man, that we might go forth, or rather (for this is the more proper expression) that we might go back to God—that putting off the old man, we might put on the new; and that as we died in Adam, so we might live in Christ, being born with Christ and crucified with him and buried with him and rising with him. For where sin abounded grace did much more abound; and if a taste condemned us, how much more does the Passion of Christ justify us? Therefore let us keep the Feast, not after the manner of a heathen festival, but after a godly sort; not after the way of the world, but in a fashion above the world; not as our own, but as belonging to him who is ours, or rather as our Master's; not as of weakness, but as of healing; not as of creation, but of re-creation.

Everything God said and did during Old Testament times pointed toward the one day when his Son would finally make his appearance on earth—born of a virgin and ready to do the work none of us could do for ourselves, namely making peace between ourselves and God.

The Mystery of God's Loving-kindness

Excerpted and adapted from a sermon by Saint John of Kronstadt (1829–1908)

Beyond all question, the mystery of godliness is great:
He appeared in a body.

1 TIMOTHY 3:16

It is on this day that, throughout the entire inhabited world, the Holy Church brings to our remembrance and observes that most majestic and sublime of mysteries: the Incarnation of God the Word from a most-pure virgin through an outpouring of, and an overshadowing by, God's Holy Spirit.

Wondrous, inexpressible, and awesome is this mystery, both for the exalted and all-contemplating celestial minds of those who dwell in the heavens: the ranks of the angels—and for the minds of men, enlightened by the Holy Spirit. Imagine: the unoriginate God from whom everything received the commencement of its existence—the angels, and the human race, and the entire world, both visible and invisible—takes a beginning in his humanity. He whom the heavens cannot contain is contained in a virginal womb. God becomes an infant and is borne upon the arms of a mother.

The science of astronomy has learned and affirms that,

in the order of creation, our earth is but a barely noticeable point; that millions of worlds around our own fill up the vastnesses of space. And, lo! this single point, this barely-noticeable globe of God's creation, being inhabited by men, has been accounted worthy of the inexpressible honor of bearing upon itself God-in-the-Flesh, the God-Man, who did deign to dwell amongst men, to teach erring mankind the knowledge of God, to work innumerable miracles of good, to preach repentance and complete forgiveness of sins; to suffer and to die as a holy sacrifice for the sins of the world, to be resurrected through the power of divinity from amongst the dead—having vanquished death, which is natural to all men—and to make a gift of resurrection to the entire human race.

Not a single one of the visible worlds, save the earth, has been deemed worthy of this greatest of all honors: for it was only upon the earth that Jesus Christ, the only-begotten of the heavenly Father, had a virgin-mother. . . . Why was the earth given such preference? Why was it only on earth that God appeared in the flesh? This is a great divine mystery, a mystery of immeasurable loving-kindness and of God's condescension to perishing mankind.

Thus, God did appear in the flesh: rejoice and be exceeding glad, O earth; rejoice and celebrate, ye earth-born. The Creator himself did come to you, in order to create you anew; to restore you, who were corrupted by transgressions. To you did he come: the almighty Physician himself—powerful to treat all the inveterate afflictions of sin—in order that he might heal all the passions of the soul and all the infirmities of the body, all of the which he truly did do, as we know from the gospel and from the history of the Church.

Thus, greet him joyfully—with pure minds and hearts, with bodies chaste and restrained by fasting and abstinence, which the Holy Church has thoughtfully instituted prior to this great feast in order to prepare us worthily to meet the heavenly Tsar, Who comes to us in order to abide in us.

He came to us with the mercy and good will of his heavenly Father—and from us he demands mercy toward our neighbors; he is the righteous Tsar—and he demands of us all righteousness; for he, too, as a man, fulfilled all righteousness (see Matthew 3:15), showing us an example and providing us with grace and the strength to carry it out. He himself did suffer for us, having borne the cross; and he taught us to deny ourselves—or our sins and our passions—and to follow after him, doing what is holy out of reverence for God (see 2 Corinthians 7:1).

He came to heal our souls, ailing from sin, and commanded all to repent; let us ever, then, be earnestly contrite, correcting ourselves and striving toward holiness and perfection. The holy Angels, at the Nativity of the God-man, did declare peace unto the world; and unto men the good will of the Heavenly Father. Let us then, ourselves, have within us a peaceful conscience, and let us be at peace with everyone, if possible. Be at peace and be holy with all, sayeth the apostle—for without this shall none see the Lord.

Amen.

God sending his Son to earth so that we could have restored fellowship with him is a wonderful mystery. Even those who know him for a lifetime can't know for sure why God extended his love to a lost and hurting humankind; they only know that he did when he sent Jesus Christ to take on human flesh and live among us.

To the Birth of Jesus

Ah, shepherds watching,
Guarding your flocks!
Behold, a Lamb born for you,
Son of our Sovereign God.

Poor and despised He comes,
Begin now guarding Him,
Lest the wolf carry Him off.
Before rejoicing in Him,
Bring me your crook, Giles.
Firmly will I grasp it,
Preventing theft of the Lamb:
See you not He is Sovereign God?

Come now, bewildered am I
By joy and sorrow joined.
If today God be born,
How can He then die?
Oh, since He is man as well.
Life in His hands will be!
In this Lamb behold,
The Son of our Sovereign God.

Why do they ask for Him
And then against Him war.
Giles, in faith it would be better
For Him to return to His land.
If by sin we are banished,
In His hand all good lies
Since to suffer He came,
This God truly sovereign.

His suffering so little troubles you:
Oh, how true of men.
When profit comes,
Evil we ignore!
Do you see He gains renown
As the Shepherd of the great flock?
Terrible it is nonetheless
That the Sovereign God should die.

—Saint Teresa of Avila (1515–1582)

NATIVITY FOUR

Prayers of Thanks and Praise for the Nativity

Classic Prayers for the Nativity

Let your goodness, Lord, appear to us, that we, made in your image, conform ourselves to it. In our own strength we cannot imitate your majesty, power, and wonder nor is it fitting for us to try. But your mercy reaches from the heavens through the clouds to the earth below. You have come to us as a small child, but you have brought us the greatest of all gifts, the gift of eternal love. Caress us with your tiny hands, embrace us with your tiny arms and pierce our hearts with your soft, sweet cries.

—Saint Bernard of Clairvaux (1090–1153)

Your nativity, O Christ our God, has shed the light of knowledge upon the world.

Through it, those who had been star-worshipers learned through a star to worship you,

O Sun of Justice, and to recognize in you the one who rises and who comes from on high.

O Lord, glory to you!

—Feast of the Nativity Liturgy

The feast day of your birth resembles You, Lord, because it brings joy to all humanity. Old people and infants alike enjoy your day. Your day is celebrated from generation to generation. Kings and emperors may pass away, and the festivals to commemorate them soon lapse. But your festival will be remembered until the end of time.

Your day is a means and a pledge of peace. At Your birth heaven and earth were reconciled, since you came from heaven to earth on that day you forgave our sins and wiped away our guilt. You gave us so many gifts on the day of your birth: A treasure chest of spiritual medicines for the sick; spiritual light for the blind; the cup of salvation for the thirsty; the bread of life for the hungry. In the winter when trees are bare, you give us the most succulent spiritual fruit. In the frost when the earth is barren, you bring new hope to our souls. In December when seeds are hidden in the soil, the staff of life springs forth from the virgin womb.

—Ephraim the Syrian (306–373)

Good Jesus, born at this time, a little child of love for us: be born in me so that I may be a little child in love with you.

—Edward Bouverie Pusey (1800–1882)

The Christ-child lay on Mary's lap,
His hair was like a light.
(Oh weary, weary was the world,
But here is all alright.)
Ah, dearest Jesus, Holy Child,
Make your bed, soft, undefiled
Within my heart, that it may be
A quiet chamber, kept for You.
My heart for very joy does leap

My lips no more can silence keep,
I must sing with joyful tongue
That sweetest ancient cradle song.

—G. K. Chesterton (1874–1936)

Loving Father, help us remember the birth of Jesus, that we may share in the song of the angels, the gladness of the shepherds, and worship of the wise men.

Close the door of hate and open the door of love all over the world. Let kindness come with every gift and good desires with every greeting. Deliver us from evil by the blessing which Christ brings, and teach us to be merry with clear hearts.

May the Christmas morning make us happy to be children, and Christmas evening bring us to our beds with grateful thoughts, forgiving and forgiven for Jesus' sake.

—Robert Louis Stevenson (1850–1894)

Where is this stupendous stranger?
Prophets, shepherds, kings advise.
Lead me to my Master's manger,
show me where my Savior lies.
O Most Mighty! O Most Holy!
Far beyond the seraph's thought:
art thou then so weak and lowly
as unheeded prophets taught?

O the magnitude of meekness!
Worth from worth immortal sprung;
O the strength of infant weakness,

if eternal is so young!
God all-bounteous, all-creative,
whom no ills from good dissuade,
is incarnate, and a native
of the very world he made.

—Christopher Smart (1722–1771)

Almighty God, who has given us your only begotten Son to take our nature upon him—and as at this time to be born of a pure virgin: grant that we, being regenerate and made your children of adoption and grace, may daily be renewed by the Holy Spirit, through our Lord Jesus Christ, who lives and reigns with you and the same Spirit, ever one God.

—The Book of Common Prayer

What is this jewel that is so precious? I can see it has been quarried not by men, but by God. It is you, dear Jesus. You have been dug from the rocks of heaven itself to be offered to me as a gift beyond price. You shine in the darkness. Every color of the rainbow can be seen within you. The whole earth is bathed in your light. Infant Jesus, by being born as man you have taken upon yourself the pain of death. But such a jewel can never be destroyed. You are immortal. And by defying your own death, you shall deliver me from death.

—The Victorines

On this day of Christmas, the Word of God, being truly God, appeared in the form of a man, and turned all adoration to himself and away from competing claims for our attention. To him, then, who through the forest of lies has beaten a clear path for us, to Christ, to the Father, and to the Holy Spirit, we offer all praise, now and forever.

—John Chrysostom (345–407)

Our God, who looked at us when we had fallen down into death and resolved to redeem us by the arrival of your only begotten Son, grant, we beg you, that those who confess his glorious Incarnation may also be admitted to the fellowship of their redeemer, through the same Jesus Christ our Lord.

—Ambrose of Milan (340–397)

As we celebrate the events commemorated by Christians during the Christmas season, we should follow the examples of believers before us and never forget to make prayer—solemn prayer of thanks and praise to our heavenly Father for the birth of our Savior—part of our celebration.

Calm on the Listening Ear of Night

Calm on the listening ear of night
Come heaven's melodious strains,
Where wild Judea stretches forth
Her silver mantled plains.
Celestial choirs from courts above
Shed sacred glories there,
And angels, with their sparkling lyres,
Make music on the air.

The answering hills of Palestine
Send back the glad reply;
And greet, from all their holy heights,
The Day-Spring from on high.
O'er the blue depths of Galilee
There comes a holier calm,
And Sharon waves, in solemn praise,
Her silent groves of palm.

"Glory to God!" the lofty strain
The realm of ether fills;
How sweeps the song of solemn joy
O'er Judah's sacred hills!
"Glory to God!" the sounding skies

Loud with their anthems ring,
"Peace to the earth; good will to men,
From heaven's eternal King!"

Light on thy hills, Jerusalem!
The Savior now is born,
And bright on Bethlehem's joyous plains
Breaks the first Christmas morn.
And brightly on Moriah's brow
Crowned with her temple spires,
Which first proclaim the newborn light,
Clothed with its orient fires.

This day shall Christian tongues be mute,
And Christian hearts be cold?
Oh, catch the anthem that from heaven
O'er Judah's mountains rolled.
When burst upon that listening night
The high and solemn lay:
"Glory to God, on earth be peace,"
Salvation comes today!

—Edmund Hamilton Sears (1810–1876)

Christmas is the day we celebrate the birth of Jesus Christ, our Lord and Savior—the day we celebrate God's keeping his promise of salvation coming to all humankind who put their faith in him.

The Joy of the Nativity

Adapted from a sermon by Saint Bernard of Clairvaux (1090–1153)

Jesus Christ, the Son of God,
is born in Bethlehem of Juda.

What heart so stony as not to be softened at these words? What soul is not melted at this voice of her Beloved? What announcement could be sweeter? What intelligence more enrapturing? Was its like ever heard before? Or when did the world ever receive such tidings?

Jesus Christ, the Son of God,
is born in Bethlehem of Juda.

O short word, telling of the Eternal Word abbreviated for us! O word full of heavenly delights! The heart is oppressed by its mellifluous sweetness, and longs to pour forth its redundant riches, but words refuse their service. So overpowering is the music of this short speech that it loses its melody if one iota is changed.

Jesus Christ, the Son of God,
is born in Bethlehem of Juda.

O Nativity of spotless sanctity! O birth honorable for the world, birth pleasing and welcome to men, because of the magnificence of the benefit it bestows; birth incomprehensible to the angels, by reason of the depth and sacredness of the mystery! In all its circumstances it is wonderful because of its singular excellence and novelty. Its precedent has not been known, nor has its like ever followed. O birth alone without sorrow, alone without shame, free from corruption, not unlocking, but consecrating the temple of the virgin's womb! O Nativity above nature, yet for the sake of nature! Surpassing it by the excellence of the miracle, repairing it by the virtue of the mystery! Who shall declare this generation? The angel announces it. Almighty Power overshadows it. The Spirit of the Most High comes upon it. The virgin believes. By faith she conceives. The virgin brings forth. The virgin remains a virgin. Who is not filled with astonishment? The Son of the Most High is born. The Son, begotten of God for all ages, is Incarnate! The Word is become an Infant! Who can sufficiently admire?

And it is not a needless Nativity, a superfluous condescension of Infinite Majesty.

Jesus Christ, the Son of God,
is born in Bethlehem of Juda.

Awake, you who lie in the dust—awake and give praise. Behold the Lord cometh with salvation. He comes with salvation, he comes with unction, He comes with glory. Jesus cannot come without salvation, Christ cannot come without unction, nor the Son of God without glory. For He Himself is salvation, He is unction, He is glory, as it is written, "A wise son is the glory of his father."

Happy the soul who has tasted this fruit of salvation, and is drawn to "run in the odor of his ointments," that she may "see his glory, the glory of the only-begotten of the Father." Take courage, you who were lost: Jesus comes to seek and save that which was lost. You sick, return to health: Christ comes to heal the contrite of heart with the unction of His mercy. Rejoice, all you who desire great things: The Son of God comes down to you that He may make you co-heirs of His Kingdom. I beseech you, then, O Lord, heal me, and I shall be healed; save me, and I shall be saved; glorify me, and I shall be glorious. Then indeed shall my soul bless the Lord, and all that is within me praise His Holy Name, when He shall have been merciful to my iniquities, have healed my infirmities, and have filled my desire with good things.

On account of these three precious gifts of salvation, unction, and glory, it is consoling to hear that Jesus Christ, the Son of God, is born. For why is He called Jesus, but because He shall save His people from their sins? Why has He willed to be named Christ, but because he will soften the yoke of His law by the unction of His grace? Why was the Son of God made man, but to make men the sons of God? Who shall resist His will? If Jesus justifies, who can condemn? If Christ heals, who can wound? If the Son of God exalts, who shall cast us down?

Since Jesus is born, let everyone rejoice whom the consciousness of sin has condemned as deserving of eternal punishment. For the compassion of Jesus exceeds all crimes, however great their number and enormity. Since Christ is born, let him rejoice who wages war with the vices inherent in our nature. No disorder of the soul, how inveterate soever, can withstand the unction which Christ brings. Since the Son of God is born, let him rejoice who desires great things, for a great reward comes. "This is the heir"; let us receive Him devoutly, "and the inheritance shall be ours." For He Who has given us His own Son, how has He not with Him given us all things? Let no one disbelieve, let no one doubt; we have a most trustworthy testimony: "The Word made flesh and dwelt among us."

The birth of Jesus Christ two thousand years ago marked the arrival of the gift God had for thousands of years promised all humankind. Because of that gift, all men and women—Jew and Gentile alike—can enjoy the forgiveness, healing, and peace Jesus brings us.

The Precious, Sweet Name of Jesus

Adapted from a sermon by Charles H. Spurgeon (1834–1892)

But after he [Joseph] had considered this, an angel of the Lord appeared to him in a dream and said, "Joseph son of David, do not be afraid to take Mary home as your wife, because what is conceived in her is from the Holy Spirit. She will give birth to a son, and you are to give him the name Jesus, because he will save his people from their sins."

MATTHEW 1:20-21

So inexpressibly fragrant is the name of Jesus that it imparts a delicious perfume to everything which comes in connection with it. Our thoughts turn to the first use of the name in connection with our Lord, when the child who was yet to be born was named Jesus. Here we find everything suggestive of comfort.

The person to whom that name was first revealed was Joseph, a carpenter, a humble man, a working man, unknown and undistinguished save by the justice of his character. To the artisan of Nazareth was the name first imparted. It is not, therefore, a title to be monopolized by the ears of princes, sages, priests, warriors or men of wealth: it is a name to be made a household word among the common people. He is the people's Christ; for of old it was said of him, "I have exalted one chosen out of the people." Let every carpenter, and every worker of every sort, rejoice with all other sorts of men in the name of Jesus. There is consolation in the messenger who made known that name to Joseph; for it was the angel of the Lord who, in the visions of the night, whispered that charming name into his ear; and henceforth angels are in league with men, and gather to one standard, moved by the same watchword as ourselves—the name of Jesus.

Did God send the name by an angel, and did the angel delight to come with it? Then is there a bond of sympathy between us and angelic spirits, and we are come this day not only "to the general assembly and the church of the first-born," but "to an innumerable company of angels," by whom that name is regarded with reverent love.

Nor is the condition of Joseph when he heard this name altogether without instruction. The angel spoke to him in a dream: that name is so soft and sweet that it breaks no man's rest, but rather yields a peace unrivaled, the peace of God. With such a dream Joseph's sleep was more blessed than his waking. The name has evermore this power, for, to those who know it, it unveils a glory brighter than dreams ever imaged. Under its power young men see visions, and old men dream dreams, and these do not mock them, but are prophecies faithful and true. The name of Jesus brings before our minds a vision of glory in the latter days when Jesus shall reign from pole to pole, and yet another vision of glory unutterable when his people shall be with him where he is.

The name of Jesus was sweet at the first, because of the

words which it accompanied; for they were meant to remove the perplexity from Joseph's mind, and some of them ran thus—"Fear not." Truly, no name can banish fear like the name of Jesus: it is the beginning of hope and the end of despair. Let but the sinner hear of "the Savior," and he forgets to die, he hopes to live; he rises out of the deadly lethargy of his hopelessness, and, looking upward, he sees a reconciled God, and fears no longer. Especially, brethren, this name is full of rare delights when we meditate upon the infinite preciousness of the person to whom it is assigned. At the time when the name was given, his full person had not been seen by mortal eyes, for he lay as yet concealed; but soon he came forth, having been born of Mary by the power of the Holy Ghost, a matchless man. He bears our nature, but not our corruption; he was made in the likeness of sinful flesh, but yet in his flesh there is no sin. This Holy One is the Son of God, and yet he is the Son of man: this surpassing excellence of nature makes his name most precious.

As beautiful and wonderful as the story of the Nativity is, there is nothing to compare with the Name above all names, Jesus Christ. It is the name through which we have forgiveness of sins, healing for our infirmities, the defeat of our fears, and future glory at the end of this age.

Nativity Poem from "At Sundown"

The Christmas of 1888

Low in the east, against a white, cold dawn,
The black-lined silhouette of the woods was drawn,
And on a wintry waste
Of frosted streams and hillsides bare and brown,
Through thin cloud-films a pallid ghost looked down,
The waning moon half-faced.

In that pale sky and sere, snow-waiting earth,
What sign was there of the immortal birth?
What herald of the One?
Lo! swift as thought the heavenly radiance came,
A rose-red splendor swept the sky like flame,
Up rolled the round, bright sun!

And all was changed. From a transfigured world
The moon's ghost fled, the smoke of home-hearths curled
Up to the still air unblown.
In Orient warmth and brightness, did that morn
O'er Nain and Nazereth, when the Christ was born,
Break fairer than our own?

The morning's promise noon and eve fulfilled
In warm, soft sky and landscape hazy-filled
And sunset fair as they;
A sweet reminder of His holiest time,
A summer-miracle in our winter clime,
God gave a perfect day.

The near was blended with the old and far,
And Bethlehem's hillside and the Magi's star
Seemed here, as there and then,—
Our homestead pine-tree was the Syrian palm,
Our heart's desire the angels' midnight psalm,
Peace, and good-will to men!

—John Greenleaf Whittier (1807–1892)

The story of the birth and infancy of Jesus Christ is as important to the believer today as it was to Mary, Joseph, the shepherds, and the magi who were there. It is to us the message of peace and good will to all men.

Wise Men Seek Him

Adapted from the works of Matthew Henry (1662–1714)

After Jesus was born in Bethlehem in Judea, during the time of King Herod, Magi from the east came to Jerusalem and asked, "Where is the one who has been born king of the Jews? We saw his star in the east and have come to worship him."

MATTHEW 2:1-2

Those who live at the greatest distance from the means of grace often use most diligence, and learn to know the most of Christ and his salvation. But no curious arts, or mere human learning, can direct men unto him. We must learn of Christ by attending to the Word of God, as a light that shineth in a dark place, and by seeking the teaching of the Holy Spirit. And those in whose hearts the day-star is risen, to give them any thing of the knowledge of Christ, make it their business to worship him. Though Herod was very old, and never had shown affection for his family, and was not himself likely to live till a new-born infant had grown up to manhood, he began to be troubled with the dread of a rival. He understood not the spiritual nature of the Messiah's kingdom. Let us beware of a dead faith. A man may be persuaded of many truths, and yet may hate them, because they interfere with his ambition, or sinful indulgences. Such a belief will make him uneasy, and the more resolved to oppose the truth and the cause of God; and he may be foolish enough to hope for success therein.

What joy these wise men felt upon this sight of the star, none know so well as those who, after a long and melancholy night of temptation and desertion, under the power of a spirit of bondage, at length receive the Spirit of adoption, witnessing with their spirits that they are the children of God. We may well think what a disappointment it was to them, when they found a cottage was his palace, and his own poor mother the only attendant he had. However, these wise men did not think themselves baffled; but having found the King they sought, they presented their gifts to him. The humble inquirer after Christ will not be stumbled at finding him and his disciples in obscure cottages, after having in vain sought them in palaces and populous cities. Is a soul busy, seeking after Christ? Would it worship him, and does it say, Alas! I am a foolish and poor creature, and have nothing to offer? Nothing! Hast thou not a heart, though unworthy of him, dark, hard, and foul? Give it to him as it is, and be willing that he use and dispose of it as it pleases him; he will take it, and will make it better, and thou shalt never repent having given it to him. He shall frame it to his own likeness, and will give thee himself, and be thine forever. The gifts the wise men presented were gold, frankincense, and myrrh. Providence sent these as a seasonable relief to Joseph and Mary in their present poor condition. Thus our heavenly Father, who knows what his children need, uses some as stewards to supply the wants of others, and can provide for them, even from the ends of the earth.

It takes wisdom to seek after Christ but humility to find him. Those who seek with humility and sincerity will find him, and when they do, they should give to him all they have, no matter how beautiful, no matter how flawed—then let him take it, mold it, and use it as he will.

Hymn for the Nativity

From Poems and Translations, *1887*

Happy night and happy silence downward softly stealing
Softly stealing over land and sea,
Stars from golden censers swing a silent eager feeling
Down on Judah, down on Galilee;
And all the wistful air, and earth, and sky,
Listened, listened for the gladness of a cry.

Holy, night, a sudden flash of light its way is winging:
Angels, angels, all above, around;
Hark, the angel voices, hark, the angel voices singing;
And the sheep are lying on the ground.
Lo, all the wistful air, and earth, and sky
Listen, listen to the gladness of the cry.

Happy night at Bethlehem; soft little hands are feeling,
Feeling in the manger with the kine:
Little hands, and eyelids closed in sleep, while
angels kneeling,
Mary, mother, hymn the Babe Divine.
Lo, all the wistful air, and earth, and sky,
Listen, listen to the gladness of the cry.

Wide, as if the light were music, flashes adoration:
Glory be to God, nor ever cease.
All the silence thrills, and speeds the message of salvation:
Peace on earth, good-will to men of peace
Lo, all the wistful air, and earth, and sky,
Listen, listen to the gladness of the cry.

Holy night, thy solemn silence evermore enfoldeth
Angel songs and peace from God on high:
Holy night, thy watcher still with faithful eye beholdeth
Wings that wave, and angel glory nigh.
Lo, hushed is strife in air, and earth, and sky,
Still thy watchers hear the gladness of the cry.

Praise Him, ye who watch the night, the silent night of ages:
Praise Him, shepherds, praise the Holy Child:
Praise Him, ye who hear the light, O praise Him,
all ye sages;
Praise Him children, praise Him meek and mild.
Lo, peace on Earth, glory to God on high,
Listen, listen to the gladness of the cry.

—Edward Thring (1821–1887)

All believers from all ages and walks of life can and should praise and thank God for the birth of the Christ two thousand years ago because this is the event that was the start of a life that changed the world: the life of Jesus Christ, which set for us the standard for godliness and holiness.

Christ in Me

Adapted from The Spirit of Prayer, *by William Law (1686–1761)*

"I have been crucified with Christ and I no longer live, but Christ lives in me. The life I live in the body, I live by faith in the Son of God, who loved me and gave himself for me."

GALATIANS 2:20

It is clear from Scripture that no one can fail to benefit from Christ's salvation unless he or she is unwilling to have it, as are all unbelievers in the world today. But if you would still further know how this great work, the birth of Christ, is to be effected in you, then let this joyful truth be told you, that this great work is already begun in every one of us.

For this holy Jesus, who is to be formed in you, who is to be the Savior and new life of your soul, who is to raise you out of the darkness of death into the light of life and give you power to become a son of God, is already within you, living, stirring, calling, knocking at the door of your heart, and wanting nothing but your own faith and good will, to have as real a birth and form in you, as he had in the Virgin Mary.

For the eternal Word, or Son of God, did not then first begin to be the Savior of the world when he was born in Bethlehem of Judea; but that Word who became man in the

Virgin Mary did, from the beginning of the world, enter as a Word of life, a seed of salvation, into the first father of mankind, was inspoken into him, as an ingrafted Word, under the name and character of a bruiser of the serpent's head.

Christ said to his disciples, "The kingdom of God is within you," meaning that the divine nature is within you, given to your first father, into the light of his life, and from him, rising up in the life of every son of Adam.

Hence also the holy Jesus is said to be the "true light that gives light to every man . . . coming into the world" (John 1:9). Not as he was born at Bethlehem, not as he had a human form upon earth; in these respects he could not be said to have been the light of every man that cometh into the world; but as he was that eternal Word, by which all things were created, which was the life and light of all things, and which had as a second creator entered again into fallen man, as a bruiser of the serpent; in this respect it was truly said of our Lord, when on earth, that he was "the true light that gives light to every man," for he was really and truly all this, as he was the Immanuel, the God with us, given unto Adam, and in him to all his offspring.

See here the beginning and glorious extent of the catholic church of Christ it takes in all the world. It is God's unlimited, universal mercy to all mankind; and every human creature, as sure as he is born of Adam, has a birth of the bruiser of the serpent within him, and so is infallibly in covenant with God through Jesus Christ.

Hence also it is, that the holy Jesus is appointed to be judge of all the world, it is because all mankind, all nations and languages have in him, and through him been put into covenant with God, and made capable of resisting the evil of their fallen nature.

Oh plain, and easy, and simple way of salvation, wanting no subtleties of art or science, no borrowed learning, no refinements of reason, but all done by the simple natural motion of every heart that truly longs after God. For no sooner is the finite desire of the creature in motion towards God, but the infinite desire of God is united with it, co-operates with it. And in this united desire of God and the creature, is the salvation and life of the soul brought forth. For the soul is shut out of God, and imprisoned in its own dark workings of flesh and blood, merely and solely, because it desires to live to the vanity of this world. This desire is its darkness, its death, its imprisonment, and separation from God.

When therefore the first spark of a desire after God arises in your soul, cherish it with all your care, give all your heart into it, it is nothing less than a touch of the divine loadstone, that is to draw you out of the vanity of time into the riches of eternity. Get up therefore and follow it as gladly, as the wise men of the East followed the star from heaven that appeared to them. It will do for you, as the star did for them. It will lead you to the birth of Jesus, not in a stable at Bethlehem in Judea, but to the birth of Jesus in the dark center of your own fallen soul.

Jesus was born in a stable in Bethlehem two thousand years ago, but the more important birth is the one he does in each of us when we through faith allow him to take up residence inside us.

Christ's Nativity

Awake, glad heart! get up and sing!
It is the birth-day of thy King.
Awake! awake!
The Sun doth shake
Light from his locks, and all the way
Breathing perfumes, doth spice the day.

Awake, awake! hark how th' wood rings;
Winds whisper, and the busy springs
A concert make;
Awake! awake!
Man is their high-priest, and should rise
To offer up the sacrifice.

I would I were some bird, or star,
Flutt'ring in woods, or lifted far
Above this inn
And road of sin!
Then either star or bird should be
Shining or singing still to thee.

I would I had in my best part
Fit rooms for thee! or that my heart

Were so clean as
Thy manger was!
But I am all filth, and obscene;
Yet, if thou wilt, thou canst make clean.

Sweet Jesu! will then. Let no more
This leper haunt and soil thy door!
Cure him, ease him,
O release him!
And let once more, by mystic birth,
The Lord of life be born in earth.

—Henry Vaughan (1621–1695)

As believers, when we celebrate Christmas, we aren't just taking part in a traditional yearly holiday festival. No, we are celebrating the birthday of our eternal Savior, our eternal Lord, our eternal King! Jesus was born in a stable, and his birth was met by the praises of angels, who sang, "Glory to God in the highest, and on earth peace to men on whom his favor rests" (Luke 2:14). Knowing what this day is about, how can we do any less?

NATIVITY FIVE

The Birth of Jesus Fulfills the Promises of God

Christ's Birth: Promises Fulfilled

Adapted from the works of Irenaeus of Lyons (115–202)

In sending Jesus Christ to be born of a virgin in the tiny town of Bethlehem, God fulfilled his promise made to Abraham that he would make his seed like the stars of heaven. Jesus did just that by being born of the virgin—Mary—who came of Abraham's seed, and setting up as lights in the world those who believe in Him, justifying the Gentiles through the same faith with Abraham.

The Bible tells us that "Abraham believed God, and it was credited to him as righteousness" (Romans 4:3). In like manner we too are justified by believing God, for a just man shall live by faith. So not through the law was the promise to Abraham, but through faith. Abraham was justified by faith, and the law is not made for the just man. So too are we justified not through the law, but through the faith of Him to whom witness was borne by the law and the prophets whom the Word of God brought to us.

And he fulfilled the promise made to David, that the Messiah would be his descendant: "The LORD declares to you that the LORD himself will establish a house for you: When your days are over and you rest with your fathers, I will raise up your offspring to succeed you, who will come from your own body, and I will establish his kingdom. He is the one who will build a house for my Name, and I will establish the throne of his kingdom forever" (2 Samuel 7:11–13).

God is humanity's glory and humanity is the vessel that receives God's action and all his wisdom and power. Just as a doctor is judged in his care for the sick, so God is revealed in his conduct with men. That is Paul's reason for saying, "For God has bound all men over to disobedience so that he may have mercy on them all" (Romans 11:32). He was speaking of all of humanity, which was disobedient to God and cast off from immortality but then who found mercy, receiving through the Son of God the adoption he brings.

If man, without being puffed up or boastful, has a right belief regarding created things and their divine Creator, who, having given them being, holds them all in his power, and if man perseveres in God's love, and in obedience and gratitude to him, he will receive greater glory from him. It will be a glory which will grow ever brighter until he takes on the likeness of the one who died for him.

He it was who took on the likeness of sinful flesh so he could condemn sin and rid the flesh of sin, as now condemned. He wanted to invite man to take on his likeness, appointing man an imitator of God, establishing man in a way of life in obedience to the Father that would lead to the vision of God, and endowing man with power to receive the Father. He is the Word of God who dwelt with man and became the Son of Man to open the way for man to receive God, for God to dwell with man, according to the will of the Father.

For this reason the Lord himself gave as the sign of our salvation the one who was born of the Virgin, Emmanuel. It was the Lord himself who saved us, for of ourselves we had no power to be saved. For this reason Paul speaks of the weakness of man, and says, "I know that nothing good lives in me" (Romans 7:18), meaning that the blessing of our salvation comes not from us but from God. Again, he says: "What a wretched man I am! Who will rescue me from this body of death?" (Romans 7:24). Then he speaks of a liberator, thanks to Jesus Christ our Lord.

Isaiah says the same: "Strengthen the feeble hands, steady the knees that give way; say to those with fearful hearts, 'Be strong, do not fear; your God will come with vengeance; with divine retribution he will come to save you" (35:3-4). This means that we could not be saved of ourselves but only with God's help. But because God fulfilled his promises to Abraham and David, we can have salvation through Jesus Christ our Lord.

On Christmas Day, we celebrate the birth of our Lord and Savior, Jesus Christ. Part of that celebration should be over the fact that our heavenly Father, who sent Jesus to earth for us, is a God who keeps all his promises.

The Birth of Our Mediator

Adapted from a sermon by John Calvin (1509–1564)

There is one God and one mediator between God and men, the man Christ Jesus, who gave himself as a ransom for all men—the testimony given in its proper time.

1 TIMOTHY 2:5-6

We know that it is our good, our joy and rest to be united with the Son of God. As he is our head and we are his body, so also from him we hold our life and our salvation and all good. We see how miserable our condition would be unless we had our refuge in him, to be maintained under his keeping.

But we could never reach so high had he not from his side approached us, which he did in his birth, when he clothed himself in our flesh and he made himself our brother. We could not now have our refuge in our Lord Jesus Christ and in his being seated at the right hand of God the Father in heavenly glory had he not humbled himself by being made mortal man and, therefore, having a condition common with us. That is also why, when he is called "Mediator between God and men," this title "man" is especially attributed to him. For the very same reason he is called "Emmanuel," or "God with us."

When we seek our Lord Jesus Christ, when we look to him as the easing of all our miseries and a sure and infallible protection, we must begin at his birth. Not only is it recited to us that he was made man like us, but that he so emptied himself that scarcely was he reputed to be of the rank of men. He was, after all, banished from every house and fellowship. There was nothing except a stable and a manger to receive him.

We now know that God displayed the infinite treasures of his goodness when he willed that his Son be humbled this way for our sakes. Let us recognize also how our Lord Jesus Christ from his birth so suffered for us that when we seek him we need not make long circuits to find him nor to be truly united to him. For this cause he willed to be subjected to every shame, in such a way that he was rejected by the rest of men.

We needn't empty ourselves to be of no value. For by nature already we find such poverty in ourselves that we will have good reason to be thoroughly dejected. But let us know of what sort we are, that we may offer ourselves to our Lord Jesus Christ in true humility and that he may recognize us and acknowledge us as his own.

However, we also have to note that, in the history that Luke records, on the one hand we learn how the Son of God emptied himself of everything for our salvation, on the other he did not fail to leave certain and infallible testimony that he was the Redeemer of the world promised from all time.

Even though he took our condition, he was able to maintain his heavenly majesty. Both sides are here shown to us, for our Lord Jesus Christ is here in a manger and he is, as it were, rejected by the world. He is in extreme poverty without any honor, without any reputation, as it were, subject to servitude. Yet he is magnified by angels from paradise, who reverence him.

To start with, an angel bears the message of his birth. Later, the same angel is accompanied by a great multitude—even an army—of angels who all appear as witnesses sent by God to show that our Lord Jesus Christ, being thus abased for the salvation of men, never ceases to be King of all the world and to have everything under his dominion.

Then the place, Bethlehem, gives proof that it was he who had been promised from all time. For the prophet Micah had spoken thus: "But you, Bethlehem Ephrathah, though you are small among the clans of Judah, out of you will come for me one who will be ruler over Israel, whose origins are from of old, from ancient times" (5:2).

We see, then, here on the one hand how our Lord Jesus Christ did not spare himself, so that we might have access to him and that we might not doubt that we are received even as his body, since he willed to be not only a mortal man clothed in our nature, but, as it were, a poor earthworm stripped of all good. May we never doubt, then, however miserable we may be, that he will keep us as his members.

On the other hand, we see him here marked by the hand of God, so that he may be received without any difficulty, as him from whom we must expect salvation, and by whom we are received into the Kingdom of God, from which we were previously banished. For we see that he has in himself a divine majesty, since the angels recognize him as their superior and their sovereign King. We ought not to doubt, when we shall be under his keeping, that he has all that is needed to maintain us. Let us know, however much he was abased, it in no wise takes away from his divine power nor hinders us from being securely under his guidance.

Now we see the summary of this history. That is, in the first place, we know that the Son of God, even our Mediator, has united himself to us in such a way that we must never doubt that we are sharers both of his life and of all his riches. Let us know also that he brought with himself to us everything that was required for our salvation.

Jesus Christ, our Lord and Savior, gave himself up as the mediator between a holy God and a sinful humankind. That giving didn't start at the Cross but in a stable in a tiny town called Bethlehem, where Jesus was born.

Born to Conquer Death

Adapted from a sermon by Dwight L. Moody (1837–1899)

"You are to give him the name Jesus, because he will save his people from their sins."

MATTHEW 1:21

When we celebrate Christmas, we celebrate one of the grandest—if not *the* grandest—events in the history of this world: the birth of Jesus Christ . . . Immanuel . . . God with us.

In the second chapter of Luke, we read of an angel appearing to some simple shepherds in the hills near Bethlehem and giving them this announcement: "I bring you good news" (verse 10).

That was good news for all people, Luke tells us, and it was this: "Today in the town of David a Savior has been born to you; he is Christ the Lord" (verse 11).

The angels came to bring the good tidings to *us*, and it was news of our own Savior. If the angels couldn't look into the future, I have no doubt that they would have thought that the world would rise up and receive Jesus as one. Instead, however, the story of Christ's birth finds not only Herod but all of Jerusalem troubled when the wise men bring the tidings into that city (see Matthew 2:3). So often, what God calls good news seems like bad news to us humans.

You don't usually have to urge people to believe good news. We like to believe good news. And while most people don't believe the good news of the announcement the angel made two thousand years ago, it is still good news today: *A Savior has been born to us today*!

The announcement of Jesus' birth was and is good news because it takes out of our way our bitterest enemies, and that includes death. Death is a terrible, bitter enemy to the whole human race. It takes our wives, our children, our loved ones, our friends, throwing a blight across the thresholds of our lives.

Death is indeed our enemy, but the gospel of Jesus Christ tells us that this horrible adversary has been conquered forever. When Christ came into the world, he met death and conquered him. That is what Paul was saying when he wrote, "Where, O death, is your victory? Where, O death, is your sting?" (1 Corinthians 15:55). The answer to that question comes down from the cross of Christ—rolling down through the centuries—"buried in the bosom of the Son of God."

He took the sting of death into his own bosom. He tasted death for every man. What is it that makes death so bitter? It is sin. And if Christ has borne the penalty of death, if he has taken our sins on himself and borne them away on the tree, we have got the victory over death. Death is a conquered enemy, and that is because sin has been conquered.

Sin is the other enemy of our souls. There was a time when I feared having to render to God an account of my sins, but did you know that the Gospel of Christ tells us that if I believe on the Lord Jesus Christ, God will, out of his love for me, take all my sins and cast them behind his back?

The devil wants to challenge you to look at the sins God has forgiven you, but when God buries your sins and forgets them, they are buried and forgotten for all of eternity. No fiend of hell, no devil, can find our sins when God buries them. When God forgives and justifies, we are forgiven and justified for all eternity. And that's all because Jesus came to defeat death and sin forever.

That's good news indeed, isn't it?

The birth of Jesus was not only the beginning of a world-changing life, but it was also the beginning of the end of death and sin, the enemies Jesus came to defeat once and for all. That is the "good news of great joy that will be for all people" that the angel announced to the shepherds.

A Christmas without Christ

From a sermon by Clovis G. Chappell (1881–1972)

There was no room for them in the inn.

Luke 2:7

Here is a story whose pathos seems to deepen with the passing of the centuries. The angel of suffering has come to Mary, and her brow is crowned with the sweet radiance of motherhood. In her arms is a little child. That Child is Heaven's King, and the King of this world, and of all worlds. It was of him that the prophet sang: "For unto us a child is born, unto us a Son is given: and the government shall be upon his shoulder: and his name shall be called Wonderful, Counselor, The Mighty God, the everlasting Father, the Prince of Peace." He is the Word made flesh that has come to dwell among us, full of grace and truth.

His birth is an event so glorious that all Heaven is athrill with the wonder of it. A star is pointing to the manger cradle with fingers of light. An angel is proclaiming the glad tidings of great joy in words that never lose their sweetness: "For there is born unto you this day in the city of David, a Savior which is Christ the Lord." A wonderful choir from the land where everybody sings is serenading our discordant world with celestial music, praising God, and saying, "Glory to God in the highest, and on earth peace!"

But the wonder of Heaven is little shared by our sin-darkened world. It is true that a few wise men are following the pointing finger of this star, and will soon come to offer their gifts of gold, frankincense, and myrrh. Also a little handful of shepherds who have heard the angel's sermon, and have believed it, are saying one to another: "Let us now go even unto Bethlehem, and see this thing which is come to pass, which the Lord has made known unto us." And they come and find the child, and finding him, they find a new day. They find Christmas with its passion for giving. Therefore they make known abroad the saying that was told them concerning this child. But the great world passes on its way with unseeing eyes. And this innkeeper who is so close to this great event, who might have had Jesus born within his own home, misses it altogether. In fact he passes through these tremendous hours as utterly unmindful as the dead that anything out of the ordinary is taking place. In his blindness he throws Heaven's supreme gift into an old outhouse, because there is no room at the inn.

Since that distant day, this Child has grown to manhood. He has spoken as never man spake. He has shown himself to be the wisdom of God and the power of God. He has gone to the cross for man's redemption. He has broken the bonds of death. He has lifted empires off their hinges and changed the whole course of human history. Today he comes to us as the Christ of experience. He accounts for all that is best and most beautiful in our world. He accounts for that which was most kingly in your father and most queenly in your mother. Millions have been able to sing of him out of their own vital experiences:

I know not how that Bethlehem's Babe
Could in the Godhead be;
I only know the Manger Child
Has brought God's life to me.

I know not how that Calvary's Cross
A world of sin could free;
I only know its matchless love
Has brought God's love to me.

I know not how that Joseph's grave
Could solve death's mystery;
I only know a living Christ,
Our immortality.

The Savior of the world, the Lord Jesus Christ, entered the world two millennia ago with little official fanfare; in fact, his mother wasn't even provided an appropriate place to give birth. But since that time, millions and millions of people have come to know him as King of Kings and Lord of Lords.

The Profound Miracle of Christ's Birth

Adapted from the works of Peter Chrysologus (406–450)

In order for me, brothers, to be able to proclaim the Nativity of the Lord in all its majesty, I need your prayers to obtain from the Lord the means to do this, that he himself put his word in the mouth of his priest, and that he who has today seen fit to enter a partnership with our flesh may not refuse to do this favor for our mouth. For we are not striving, brothers, to reveal the indescribable mystery of the divine generation, but we are eager to announce the great and wonderful joy of our salvation, just as the angel said: "I bring you good news of great joy that will be for all the people" (Luke 2:10).

May this conception, may this birth frighten no one today, brothers. For when virginity conceives, when purity gives birth, it is the power of God and not pleasure that is clearly at work. Listen to the angel's words: "The Holy Spirit will come upon you, and the power of the Most High will overshadow you" (Luke 1:35).

What is being accomplished, brothers, is something divine and not human. Never is the virginity naked which is adorned with the eternal cloak of its purity. The angel comes as forerunner to the dwelling place of chastity, in order to prepare the royal court for the King, the temple for God, and the marriage chamber for the heavenly Bridegroom. For when the Lord was born, virginity was not lost but consecrated, which itself bore the Bridegroom and Guardian of its purity.

Mary offers faithful service: pregnant, yet a virgin; a virgin, yet a mother, for it was barrenness, not purity, that she lacked. There stand at hand sanctity, sincerity, modesty, chastity, integrity, and faith, and all the virtues were present together, so that the fearless maidservant would carry her Creator in her womb, and, while being the champion of her sex, she would know no pain or groans in giving birth to the Power of heaven.

Blessed is that fruitfulness which both acquired the honor of motherhood and did not lose the prize of chastity. Therefore, he does not disdain to inhabit what he deigned to fashion; he does not think that it is undignified for him to touch flesh since he had handled it in the past with his heavenly hand when it was in the form of dust.

He has come to your face, O man, because you were unable to reach his face, and he who was invisible has become visible for your redemption. The One besought by your ancestors has come. Listen to the voice of one who cries out: "Show your face, and we shall be saved." The witness of innocence and defender of purity stands at hand and does not grieve that he has lost his bride, but exults in having recognized the Lord; he follows, not as a husband, but as a servant, and he rejoices that he is paying homage to the One whom he observes all the angels serving.

So, at the time of his birth, Christ, through whom every place was created, finds no place in the inn; and he who is Lord of all the world is born as though a foreigner, to enable us to be citizens whose homeland is heaven. He is wrapped in swaddling clothes in order to restore in his own body the unity of the human race that had been rent asunder, and bring to the Kingdom of heaven the garment of immortality whole and entire, resplendent with the purple color of his blood. He is born, brothers, in order to improve the very nature which the first human being had corrupted. He lies in swaddling clothes, but he reigns in heaven; he rests humbly in a cradle, but he thunders amid the clouds; he is placed in a manger, because it is evident that "all flesh is grass," as Isaiah says. This is the grass, brothers, whose blossom is transformed into heavenly Bread, and by feasting on it we reach life eternal.

The story of the Nativity is one of miracle after miracle, all with the purpose of bringing redemption to a humanity that could do nothing to save itself. God wanted his people to understand that he and he alone could finish his plan of redemption and salvation.

The Sign Is a Baby

By E. Stanley Jones (1884–1973)

"This will be a sign to you: You will find a baby wrapped in cloths and lying in a manger."

LUKE 2:12

On the first Christmas morning the announcement was made: "And this shall be a sign to you; you shall find the baby." The sign was a baby—a fact; an embodied fact. This is the key to the whole of Christianity: it began as an embodied fact. It must continue as an embodied fact.

India would have said, "You shall find a mystic light—that shall be the sign." China would have said, "You shall find a correct code of morality." Greece would have said, "You shall find a philosophical conception." But the gospel said, "You shall find the baby." The mystic light, the correct code, the philosophical conception, and very much more, have come together in an embodied Person. Religion was now realization.

He became the reconciling place where opposites met. He was the meeting place of God and man. Man the aspiring and God the inspiring meet in Him. Heaven and earth came together and are forever reconciled. The material and the spiritual after their long divorce have in Him found their reconciliation. The natural and the supernatural blend into one in His life—you cannot tell where one ends and the other begins. The passive and the militant are so one in Him that He is militantly passive and passively militant. The gentle qualities of womanhood and the sterner qualities of manhood so mingle that both men and women see in Him their ideal—and the revelation of the Fatherhood and the Motherhood of God. The activism of the West and the meditative passivism of the East come together in Him and are forever reconciled. The new individual, born from above, and the new society—the Kingdom of God on earth—are both offered to us in Him. The sign is a fact. And thus it had to be: The weeping child would not be satisfied with the idea of motherhood—it wants a mother! We cannot be satisfied with the idea of salvation—we need a Savior!

O Christ, since the sign must be an embodied fact, help me this day to embody victorious living, and may this be my total life. Amen.

During the Christmas season, we can celebrate the historical fact of the birth of the Lord Jesus Christ. But it doesn't stop there; during the rest of the year, we also have the privilege of living our lives victoriously through what Jesus has done for us.

Entering in at the Lowly Doors

By John Henry Jowett (1864–1923)

"Unto us a Child is born."

ISAIAH 9:6, KJV

How gentle the coming! Who would have had sufficient daring of imagination to conceive that God Almighty would have appeared among men as a little child? We should have conceived something sensational, phenomenal, catastrophic, appalling! The most awful of the natural elements would have formed his retinue, and men would be chilled and frozen with fear. But he came as a little child. The great God "emptied himself"; he let in the light as our eyes were able to bear it.

"Unto us a Son is given." And that is the superlative gift! The love that bestows such a gift is all-complete and gracious. And the Son is given in order that we may all be born into sonship. It is the Son's ministry to make sons. "Now are we the sons of God," and we are of his creation.

Lord, I would serve, and be a son; dismiss me not, I pray.

"Good will toward men."

LUKE 2:14, KJV

Heavens are not filled with hostility. The sky does not express a frown. When I look up I do not contemplate a face of brass, but the face of infinite good will. Yet when I was a child, many a picture has made me think of God as suspicious, inhumanly watchful, always looking round the corner to catch me at the fall. That "eye," placed in the sky of many a picture, and placed there to represent God, filled my heart with a chilling fear.

That God was to me a magnified policeman, watching for wrong-doers, and ever ready for the infliction of punishment. It was all a frightful perversion of the gracious teaching of Jesus.

Heaven overflows with good will toward men! Our God not only wishes good, he wills it. "He gave his only begotten Son" as the sacred expression of his infinite good will. He has good will toward thee and me, and mine and thine. Let that holy thought make our Christmas cheer.

God sent us his son out of his own love and good will toward us. For that reason, we can't help but be cheered during the season in which we celebrate and commemorate the birth of our Lord Jesus Christ.

The Wonder of His Name

From Open Treasures, *by Francis Ridley Havergal (1836–1879)*

"For unto us a Child is born, unto us a Son is given;
and the government will be upon His shoulder.
And His name will be called Wonderful."

ISAIAH 9:6, NKJV

All the other names of Jesus are nouns. But here is a name that is an adjective; so we may use it not only as a name by itself, but as an adjective to all His other names; and the more we know Him and love Him the more we shall delight in this.

If we know Jesus as our Savior at all, we shall be quite sure that He is a Wonderful Savior. And if we grow in grace and in the knowledge of our Lord and Savior Jesus Christ, we shall find more and more, year by year, and even day by day, what a Wonderful Friend, and Wonderful Gift, and Wonderful High Priest, and Wonderful everything else He is.

When you see a wonderful sight, don't you always want others to see it first thing? And if you cannot bring them to see it, don't you want to tell about it, try to give them an idea of it? So I think one proof that we have really found Jesus is that we shall want others to come and see what a Wonderful

Savior we have found. Jesus is Wonderful in what He is. Even the angels must have wondered to see the Son of God, whom they all worship, lying in a manger as a little baby. But I think they must have wondered more still when they saw "Him taken and by wicked hands crucified and slain." They must have marveled indeed then at the love of Christ which passeth knowledge, yet He was not dying for them but for you, so you may say, "Thy love to *me* was wonderful."

Everything that He did was wonderful. Isaiah said that many should be astonished at Him; and I want you to see how exactly that was fulfilled. Look in the first seven chapters of Mark, and you will see it five times mentioned that they were astonished or amazed at Him. And His words were not less wonderful. Look in the fourth chapter of Luke, and you will see how even those who did not love Him wondered, and were astonished and amazed at His words. If we wonder at His gracious words to us now, how much more shall we wonder when we see Him on the throne of His glory, and hear His own voice.

O Bringer of Salvation, who wondrously hast wrought,
Thyself the revelation of love beyond our thought:
We worship Thee, we bless Thee, to Thee alone we sing;
We praise Thee, and confess Thee, our gracious
Lord and King!

Even before he was born, Jesus was called "Savior." But centuries before that, as Isaiah foretold the circumstances surrounding his birth, Jesus was called "Wonderful." As you look at the things Jesus said and did when he was on earth, as well as the things he does for you now, you can't help but agree that he is "Wonderful."

NATIVITY SIX

Humble Beginnings to Reach All of Humanity

The Creator of the Universe . . . Surrounded by Mud and Clay

Excerpted and adapted from a sermon by Saint Jerome (341–420)

While they were there, the time came for the baby to be born, and she gave birth to her firstborn, a son. She wrapped him in cloths and placed him in a manger, because there was no room for them in the inn.

LUKE 2:6-7

"She . . . placed him in a manger." Why in a manger?

Because there was no room for them in the inn.

Jewish unbelief had overflowed into everything in those days, and Jesus could find no room in the Holy of Holies, which shone with gold, precious stones, pure silk, and silver. He was not born in the midst of gold and riches, but in a stable in the midst of dung (wherever there is a stable, there is also dung). But in a way that is fitting because the sins he came to deliver us from are filthier than dung. He is born on a dunghill in order to lift up those who come from it. As the psalmist wrote, "He raiseth up the poor out of the dust, and lifteth the needy out of the dunghill" (Psalm 113:7, KJV). Job, too, sat and afterwards was crowned.

There was no room for them in the inn.

The poor should take great comfort from this. Joseph and Mary, the mother of the Lord, had no servant boy, no maidservant. From Nazareth in Galilee, they come all alone; they own no work animals; they are their own masters and servants. Here is a new thought. They go to the wayside inn, not into the city, for poverty is too timid to venture among the rich.

Note the extent of their poverty. They go to a wayside inn. Holy Scripture did not say that the inn was on the road, but on a wayside off the road, not on it, but beyond it; not on the way of the Law, but on the byway of the Gospel, on the byroad. There was no other place unoccupied for the birth of the Savior except a manger, a manger to which were tethered cattle and donkeys. O, if only I were permitted to see that manger in which the Lord lay!

Now, as an honor to Christ, we have taken away the manger of clay and have replaced it with a crib of silver, but more precious to me is the one that has been removed. Silver and gold are appropriate for unbelievers, but Christian faith is worthy of the manger that is made of clay. He who was born in that manger cared nothing for gold and silver. I do not find fault with those who made the change in the cause of honor (nor do I look with disfavor upon those in the Temple who made vessels of gold), but I marvel at the Lord, the Creator of the universe, who is born, not surrounded by gold and silver, but by mud and clay.

Since we have heard the Babe crying in the manger and have adored him there, let us continue our adoration of him today. Let us pick him up in our arms and adore him as the Son of God. Mighty God who for so long a time thundered in heaven and did not redeem humanity, cries and as a babe redeems him.

Why do I say all this?

Because pride never brings salvation, but humility does. As long as the Son of God was in heaven, he was not adored. He descends to earth and is adored. He had beneath him the sun, the moon, the angels, and he was not adored; on earth, he is born perfect man, a whole man, to heal the whole world.

That Jesus spent the first hours of his earthly life in a manger shows us how far he was willing to go to humble himself on our behalf. He was worthy as an infant of being placed in the holiest place on earth, but his Father chose to begin his life in a stable.

Mary and Elizabeth

Adapted from the writings of Ambrose of Milan (340–397)

At that time Mary got ready and hurried to a town in the hill country of Judea, where she entered Zechariah's home and greeted Elizabeth. When Elizabeth heard Mary's greeting, the baby leaped in her womb, and Elizabeth was filled with the Holy Spirit.

LUKE 1:39-41

When the angel revealed his message to the Virgin Mary he gave her a sign to win her trust. He told her of the motherhood of an old and barren woman to show that God is able to do all that he wills.

When Mary hears this, she sets out for the hill country. She does not disbelieve God's word; she feels no uncertainty over the message or doubt about the sign. She goes eager in purpose, dutiful in conscience, hastening for joy.

Filled with God, where would she hasten but to the heights? The Holy Spirit does not proceed by slow, laborious efforts. Quickly, too, the blessings of her coming and the Lord's presence are made clear: As soon as Elizabeth heard Mary's greeting, the child leapt in her womb, and she was filled with the Holy Spirit.

Notice the contrast and the choice of words. Elizabeth is the first to hear Mary's voice, but John is the first to be aware of grace. She hears with the ears of the body, but he leaps for joy at the meaning of the mystery. She is aware of Mary's presence, but he is aware of the Lord's: a woman aware of a woman's presence, the forerunner aware of the pledge of our salvation. The women speak of the grace they have received while the children are active in secret, unfolding the mystery of love with the help of their mothers, who prophesy by the spirit of their sons.

The child leaps in the womb; the mother is filled with the Holy Spirit, but not before her son. Once the son has been filled with the Holy Spirit, he fills his mother with the same Spirit. John leaps for joy, and the spirit of Mary rejoices in her turn. When John leaps for joy, Elizabeth is filled with the Holy Spirit, but we know that though Mary's spirit rejoices, she does not need to be filled with the Holy Spirit. Her son, who is beyond our understanding, is active in his mother in a way beyond our understanding. Elizabeth is filled with the Holy Spirit after conceiving John, while Mary is filled with the Holy Spirit before conceiving the Lord. Elizabeth says: Blessed are you because you have believed.

You also are blessed because you have heard and believed. A soul that believes both conceives and brings forth the Word of God and acknowledges his works.

Let Mary's soul be in each of you to proclaim the greatness of the Lord. Let her spirit be in each to rejoice in the Lord. Christ has only one mother in the flesh, but we all bring forth Christ in faith. Every soul receives the Word of God if only it keeps chaste, remaining pure and free from sin, its modesty undefiled. The soul that succeeds in this proclaims the greatness of the Lord, just as Mary's soul magnified the Lord and her spirit rejoiced in God her Savior. In another place we read: Magnify the Lord with me. The Lord is magnified, not because the human voice can add anything to God but because he is magnified within us. Christ is the image of God, and if the soul does what is right and holy, it magnifies that image of God, in whose likeness it was created and, in magnifying the image of God, the soul has a share in its greatness and is exalted.

Mary the mother of Jesus is an example of the kind of faith he wants each and every one of us to have, both during the Christmas season and the rest of the year—a faith that simply takes God at his word and believes that he keeps all his promises.

The Angels' Christmas Message: Do Not Be Afraid!

Adapted from a sermon by Theodore Christlieb (1833–1889)

The angel said to them, "Do not be afraid. I bring you good news of great joy that will be for all the people. Today in the town of David a Savior has been born to you; he is Christ the Lord."

LUKE 2:10-11

If as we have heard in our Christmas Gospel the shepherds of Bethlehem were "sore afraid" before that first Christmas sermon had been preached to them, what a happy introduction did the angel-preacher give it in accents which resounded in their listening ears from out his sphere of light: *Do not be afraid. I bring you good news of great joy that will be for all people.*

We can readily comprehend the "fear" with which that sudden splendor, breaking on their midnight darkness, must have filled those poor shepherds. It is a hindrance to their Christmas joy, which the angel would fain remove by this exordium.

And surely such instinctive fear and trembling, whenever some pure visitant from the world of light has drawn near to any child of man, has had a deep ground in human nature itself. Was not this the case with our first parents in Paradise? And has not such fear ever since, as then, connected with the thought and sense of sin? Oh yes, our grievous fall, our utter ruin under the pressure of divine wrath and that "fear of death" which all life through makes us "subject to bondage," brings with it the result that every ordinary human being must tremble in his inmost soul, when the light of any pure and sinless essence first shines around him. How sweet, how pleasant, then, to such, must be those opening words: *Do not be afraid*!

Fear is still the mournful inheritance of many a professed Christian. What is it that, despite all the magnificence of outward jubilation, dries up the sources in unnumbered hearts of all true inward Christmas joy? Is it not in many a case the secret fear of God's just judgment to come, for which one knows himself to be not prepared, or anxious forebodings of some future discovery that makes themselves inwardly felt and heard among the tumultuous hurries of a worldly life? Is it not a trembling glance at the years gone by, with their various burdens, or the weeks of this year now drawing to a close, or the immediate future, big it may be with fears and sorrow for ourselves or others who are near and dear to us?

So many, many causes of unrest and apprehension make Christmas Eve and its lights to shine too often upon anxious faces. All this our angel preacher meets in these opening words: *Do not be afraid*. It is as if he would say: Enough of fears and doubt, poor earth, and you poor trembling children of men! Your deepest ground for fear is taken away by him who comes as the Prince of Peace! Fear not! A remedy that is all divine is provided for your malady, whatsoever it may be. The oldest and most hardened sinner need not now sink back in despair. All may yet be forgiven or repaired, if only you will welcome this Infant to the manger. Oh let your fear be turned to gladness, for *I bring you good news of great joy that will be for all the people*. Who, after such an introduction as this, is not eager to hear the good news themselves?

If I say to a trustful child, "I have something very good to give you," the little eyes begin to sparkle, the little frame to quiver with joy, as it reaches out a hand for the unknown present. Such joyful expectation the angel would excite in these poor shepherds now. And never was a message that so well deserved the name of Good Tidings as that he now brings them. To a world of sinners its Redeemer is come; in the shadow of death life's light is shining! To the angel himself it is infinite happiness to be the bearer of such good news. He would fain infuse his gladness into us, drawn from the purest, fullest fount of joy. Abraham, David, and all the prophets have had foretastes of it in years gone by; how many myriads of Christian souls will taste its sweetness in years to come! And not those only; the joy shall be "great" to "all the people."

"To all the people": to the sons of Israel first, high and low, and then to all nations throughout the world. And the joy is one and the same to all. You prepare at Christmas different presents, for the little ones one sort, for older children another, and yet other kinds for parents and old people. But it is not so with this highest gift, of which the angel here speaks! It is one and the same great gift for all, for young and old, for rich and poor, for the shepherds at Bethlehem, for you and me. And all that this message requires of you is simple, thankful, expectant joy! At other times other things are required, but only grateful gladness now. Will you not yield it? Or does the gift appear too great for your acceptance, too good to be really meant for you?

Some years ago, a packet reached a struggling pastor in a Bohemian village. It contained a considerable sum of money towards the building of a church, and you, of this congregation, had sent it. It seemed to the good man at first too much to be meant for him, or for him to accept. But when he had opened your pastor's letter, and read the friendly cheering words which explained all to him, and made him ashamed of his previous incredulity, he burst into tears of joy and gratitude, and sent us back a warm thanksgiving.

So, Christian doubter, let it be with you now. This phrase "all the people" involves your name. Open then the letter, and see what it tells you.

Here's the great news of joy for each of us: Jesus Christ came to earth not just for humankind as a whole but for each and every one of us as individuals. Though we were once sinners on our way to eternal separation from God, we can live a life free of fear, knowing that because of his Son we are acceptable in his sight.

Joseph

Adapted from the writings of Alexander Whyte (1837–1921)

Because Joseph her husband was a righteous man and did not want to expose her to public disgrace, he had in mind to divorce her quietly. But after he had considered this, an angel of the Lord appeared to him in a dream and said, "Joseph son of David, do not be afraid to take Mary home as your wife, because what is conceived in her is from the Holy Spirit. She will give birth to a son, and you are to give him the name Jesus, because he will save his people from their sins."

MATTHEW 1:19-21

Of the two gospels that tell us anything about the birth of Christ, Matthew alone tells us Joseph's part in all this transaction. As we read the evangelist's account of that time, we see clearly that Joseph's cross was scarcely, if any, less heavy than Mary's. His heart was broken with this terrible catastrophe, but there was only one course left open to him. Consummate the marriage he could not, but neither could he consent to make Mary a public, far less a fatal, example, and there was only left to him the sad enough step of canceling the espousal, putting her away privately.

Joseph's heart, as you can well conceive, was torn in two, for Mary had been the woman of all women to him; she had been in his eyes the lily among thorns. And now to have to think of her, to have to treat her as a poisonous weed. The thought of it drove him mad. "How shall I give thee up, Ephraim! How shall I deliver thee, Israel? How shall I make thee as Admah? How shall I set thee as Zeboim? Mine heart is turned within me: my repentings are kindled together."

Oh why is it that whosoever comes near Jesus Christ has always to drink such a cup of sorrow? Truly, truly, they who are brother, or sister, or mother to him, must take up their cross daily! "These are they who go up through great tribulation."

Amid these circumstances, if thus indeed they came about, what a journey that must have been for Mary from Nazareth to Hebron, and occupied with what thoughts! As she journeyed up through the land of Judah what a glorious past would rise up upon her devout and well-stored mind, but oh, my brethren, what an unknown future in that whole land lay before that lonely maiden!

For she would pass through Jerusalem, and no doubt she tarried in the city for a night that she might rest herself and worship, and restore her heart in the Temple service. She may have crossed Olivet as the sun was setting, she may have knelt at even in Gethsemane: and she may have turned aside to look on the city from Calvary.

If I am right in my reading of her history, and if Joseph and Mary had parted before she left Nazareth in haste, what a cross she must have carried through all these scenes! Only two besides God knew the truth about Mary—an angel in heaven and her own heart upon earth. And then it was that

Mary sought the hill country of Judah in such haste, hoping there to find one who would receive her word, and understand her case. As she sped on, Mary must have recalled and repeated many happy Scriptures, well-known about indeed, but till then little understood.

The husbandmen and vinedressers saw passing them in those days, a Galilean maiden who seemed to see nothing and hear nothing as she hastened southwards. Only she would be overheard, as one communing with her own heart, saying to herself: "Commit thy way unto the Lord; trust also in him; and he shall bring it to pass. And he shall bring forth thy righteousness as the light, and thy judgment as the noonday." And again, "How great is thy goodness which thou hast laid up for them that fear thee: which thou hast wrought for them that trust in thee before the sons of men! Thou shalt hide them in the secret of thy presence from the pride of man: thou shalt keep them secretly in a pavilion from the strife of tongues." And such a pavilion Mary sought, and for a season found, in the remote and retired household of Zacharias and Elisabeth.

The meeting of Mary and Elisabeth is one of the most beautiful episodes in Holy Scripture. And it teaches us a happy truth that we have often had some experience of ourselves—how the crosses and trials of our lives are relieved, and how faith and hope and love and joy are revived and increased as one gracious heart meets with another.

Sweet as it is to linger in Hebron with Elisabeth and Mary, yet somehow my heart always draws back to Joseph in desolate and darkened Nazareth. "The absent are dear, just as the dead are perfect." And Mary's dear image became to Joseph dearer still when he could no longer see her face or hear her voice. Nazareth was empty to Joseph, it was worse than empty; it was a city of sepulchres to him in which he sought for death and could not find it. All the weary week his bitterness increased, and when, as his wont was, he went up to the synagogue on the Sabbath day, that only made him feel his loneliness and distress the more.

Mary's sweet presence had often made that holy place still holier to him, and her voice in the psalms had often been as when an angel sings. On one of those Sabbaths which the exiled Virgin was spending with Elisabeth at Hebron, Joseph went up again to the sanctuary of God in Nazareth, seeking, as so many others were no doubt seeking, to hide his grief with God and to commit his way to him. And this, shall I suppose, was the Scripture appointed to be read in the synagogue that day:

Ask thee a sign of the Lord thy God; ask it either in the depth, or in the height above. . . .

Therefore the Lord himself shall give you a sign: Behold a virgin shall conceive, and bear a son, and shall call his name Immanuel.

Joseph heard Isaiah speak that day as no man in the house of Israel had ever heard before. God spake that day in Joseph's heavy heart. He rose up and found himself at home, a man astonied. When he laid himself down to sleep that night, his pillow became a stone under his head. Not that he was cast out, but that he had cast out another, and she the best of God's creatures he had ever known! She, perhaps—how shall he utter it even to himself at midnight—she, perhaps, the Virgin Mother of King Messiah. A better mother he could not have. And so, speaking to himself, afraid at what he said to himself, weary with a week's labors, aged with many weeks of uttermost sorrow, Joseph fell asleep. Then a thing was secretly brought to him, and his ear received a little thereof. In thoughts from the visions of the night, when deep sleep falleth on men, then a spirit passed before his face; there was silence, and the sleeper heard a voice saying: "Joseph, thou son of David, fear not to take unto thee Mary, thy wife: for that which is conceived in her is of the Holy Ghost. And she shall bring forth a son, and thou shalt call his name Jesus: for he shall save his people from their sins."

Gabriel had come in the name of God, to reassure the despairing heart of the bridegroom, to demand of him the consummation of the broken-off marriage, and to announce the Incarnation of the Son of God; he had even told Joseph the Heaven-given name of the divine Child who was thus committed to his fatherly care.

The story of the Nativity includes the struggles of a young man named Joseph, who needed God to assure him and instruct him in the way he was to go. God gave him those things, and because he was an obedient, righteous man, he had the privilege of giving Jesus Christ fatherly care as he was growing up.

Mary and Joseph's part in the Nativity story was one of obedience, one of being ready to adapt and adjust to the plan God had for bringing the Christ child into the world. We should be willing to show that same kind of obedience—and flexibility—as we take him to the world around us.

Good News from Bethlehem

Adapted from the works of Horatius Bonar (1808–1889)

There was nothing great about Bethlehem. It was "little among the thousands of Judah" (Micah 5:2, KJV); perhaps but a shepherd-village or small market town; yet there the great purpose of God became a *fact*; "The Word was made flesh."

It is in *facts* that God's purposes come to us, that we may take hold of them as real things. It is into *facts* that God translates his truth, that it may be visible, audible, tangible. It is in *facts* (as in so many seeds) that God embodies his good news, that a little child may grasp them in his hand. So was it with the miracle of our text. God took his eternal purpose and dropped it over Bethlehem in the form of a fact, a little fragment of human history. Over earth, the first promise had been hovering, for four thousand years, till at last it rested over Bethlehem, as if it said, "This is my rest; here will I dwell."

The city is poor rather than rich. It is not without its attractions; but these are of the more homely kind. Its scenes are not stately; its hills are not lofty; its plains are not wide; its slopes are rocky; it is not like the city of the Great King, beautiful for situation, the joy of the whole earth. Yet there "the Word was made flesh."

It has no palace nor temple; only an inn for the travelers passing between Hebron and Jerusalem; its dwellers are not priests nor princes; it is not a sacred city, and is but little noted in history. Yet there, not at Jerusalem, "the Word was made flesh."

But its lowliness makes it more suitable as the birthplace of him who, though he was rich, for our sakes became poor. And all about it seems to suit him too. It is "the house of bread," fit dwelling for him who is "the bread of God." Its old name was Ephratah, "the fruitful," as if pointing to the fruitful one. At its gate is the well of David; and not far off are the pools of Solomon, which pour their water into Jerusalem, telling us of the living water, and the river whose streams make glad the city of our God. The gardens of Solomon are also hard by, speaking to us not only of "the garden of the Lord," and the second Adam, and the tree of life, but giving us the earthly scenes (which are the patterns of the heavenly) which the "Song of songs" describes (see Song of Songs 2:12-13).

In walking through its streets, or wandering over its heights, one seems to read text after text, written, not with an iron, but a golden pen, upon its hills and rocks. "Unto us a Child is born," seems inscribed on one; "Unto us a Son is given," on another; "Unto you is born a Savior," on a third; "Glory to God in the highest," on a fourth; the name of Jesus upon all. The city is not now what it was, yet there it sits upon the northern face of its old height; the one town in Palestine still possessed exclusively by those who call themselves by the name of Christ.

Bethlehem is not named in our text; but you cannot read the verse without being transported to that city. "In the beginning was the Word," carries you up into heaven, and back into past infinity. "The Word was made flesh," brings you down to earth and the finite things of time; to the manger, and the stable, and "the young Child." The shepherds are gone; the wise men have departed to their own country; the glory has passed up again into heaven; the angels have left; the song of the plain has ceased; the star has disappeared—the star of which Balaam spoke, as yet to sparkle somewhere in these eastern heavens, and which Micah may be said to have fixed and hung over the city, when he named the name of Bethlehem as the birthplace of the coming King—but the city itself is still there, rooted to its old spot; not, like Rachel's tomb hard; by, a memorial of death and sorrow, but a remembrance of joy and peace, a witness of the everlasting life which came down from heaven.

At Bethlehem our world's history begins. All before and after the birth of the young child takes its color from that event. As the tree, rising from a small root or seed, spreads its branches, and with them its leaves, its blossoms, its fruit, its shade, north, south, east, and west; so has this obscure birth influenced all history, sacred and secular, before and behind. That history is an infinite coil of events, interwoven in endless intricacies, apparently with a thousand broken ends; now upward, now downward, now backward, now forward; but the raveled coil is *one,* and its center is Bethlehem. The young Child there is the interpreter of all its mysteries. As he is "the beginning of the creation of God," the "first-begotten of the dead," so is he the beginning and ending, the center and circumference of human history. "Christ is all and in all," and as such, from the manger to the throne, he is the incarnation of Jehovah's purposes, the interpretation of the divine actings, and the revelation of the heavenly mysteries.

Bethlehem, the birthplace of the Lord Jesus Christ, wasn't more than a stopover on the way to more important places, but it was the perfect town for the birth of One who while he was rich became poor for our sakes.

Wonderful

Adapted from a work by Billy Sunday (1862–1935)

His name shall be called Wonderful.

ISAIAH 9:6, KJV

In olden times all names meant something, and this is still the case among Indians. Whenever you know an Indian's name and the meaning of it, you know something about the Indian. Such names as Kill Deer, Eagle Eye, Buffalo Face, and Sitting Bull tell us something about the men who possessed them.

This tendency to use names that are expressive still crops out in camp life, and whenever men are thrown together in an unconventional way. In mining, military, and lumber camps nearly every man has a nickname that indicates some peculiarity or trait of character. Usually a man's nickname is nearer the real man than his right name.

All of our family names today had their origin in something that meant something. All Bible names have a meaning, and when you read the Scriptures it will always help you to a better understanding of their meaning to look up the definition of all proper names.

There are two hundred and fifty-six names given in

the Bible for the Lord Jesus Christ, and I suppose this was because he was infinitely beyond all that any one name could express.

Of the many names given to Christ it is my purpose at this time to briefly consider this one: "His name shall be called Wonderful." Let us look into it somewhat and see whether he was true to the name given him in a prophecy eight hundred years before he was born. Does the name fit him? Is it such a name as he ought to have?

Wonderful means something that is transcendently beyond the common; something that is away beyond the ordinary. It means something that is altogether unlike anything else. We say that Yellowstone Park, Niagara Falls, and the Grand Canyon are wonderful because there is nothing else like them.

Let us see whether Jesus was true to his name.

His birth was wonderful, for no other ever occurred that was like it. It was wonderful in that he had but one human parent, and so inherited the nature of man and the nature of God. He came to be the Prince of princes, and the King of kings, and yet his birth was not looked forward to in glad expectation, as the birth of a prince usually is in the royal palace, and celebrated with marked expressions of joy all over the country, as has repeatedly happened within the recollection of many who are here.

There was no room for him at the inn, and he had to be born in a stable, and cradled in a manger, and yet angels proclaimed his birth with joy from the sky, to a few humble shepherds in sheepskin coats, who were watching their flocks by night.

Mark how he might have come with all the pomp and glory of the upper world. It would have been a great condescension for him to have been born in a palace, rocked in a golden cradle and fed with golden spoons, and to have had the angels come down and be his nurses. But he gave up all the glory of that world, and was born of a poor woman, and his cradle was a manger.

Think what he had come for. He had come to bless, and not to curse; to lift up, and not to cast down. He had come to seek and to save that which was lost. To give sight to the blind; to open prison doors and set captives free; to reveal the Father's love; to give rest to the weary; to be a blessing to the whole world, and yet there was no room for him.

He came to do all that. Do you have room for him in your heart?

Isaiah tells us that Jesus' name would be called "Wonderful." Indeed, everything Jesus did during his time on earth was wonderful, meaning that it transcended all else. That all started with his birth, which while it was in humble circumstances (in a stable or, more likely, a cave), was truly wonderful (announced by holy angels of God).

Christmas Day: A Taste of Eternity

Adapted from the works of Frederick Denison Maurice (1805–1872)

We have all heard and seen that Christmas day is a good day, a day when children and parents, brothers and sisters, should meet together and rejoice; they have, accordingly, met and kept a holiday. As long as they remembered that they were kinsfolk, and liked coming together for the sake of greeting old friends and looking at the happy faces of children, they had the savor of Christmas day in them, even though they might not always recollect in whose name they were assembled, and what his coming into the world had to do with their good fellowship.

But by degrees, the song, and the cup, and the dance, which were signs of the pleasure that friends and brothers had in seeing one another, were more thought of than their friendship and their brotherhood; then the joy wasted away, and went so much the faster because they were trying to invent ways of keeping it up. If we care about nothing but ourselves, we shall not be merry at Christmas time, or at any other time.

And therefore, brethren, I do not know what those mean who say that we are to be good Christians in our hearts, but are not to think about Christmas day. That seems to me like saying that we are to be very good Christians for ourselves, but that we are not to care whether our neighbors have any share in the blessing or not. Now how a man can be a good Christian and only be concerned about himself, I do not know. These days are witnesses to all men, everywhere, young and old, rich and poor, of a blessing which God has bestowed upon them: if there be no such blessing we ought to say so plainly; but if there be, it is a base and miserable thing not to like the plain, simple testimonies of it which come down from generation to generation, and which all alike may own and rejoice in whether they have book-learning or no.

And mark this, also, brethren: They who would cheat us of these days and send us to a book, though it be the best book in the world, for all our teaching, soon forget that our faith is not in a book, but in him of whom the book speaks. They forget that the Word is a living person, and that he was made flesh and dwelt among us. These days bear witness of that truth—bless God for them.

Yes, bless God for them! For he is a liar who says that the words which Saint John speaks to us today are not as fresh, as living, as necessary now as they were when he first wrote them down. It may be, brethren, that easy, comfortable people make less of Christmas day than they once did.

We do not keep Christmas in the bright, sunny time of the year, but in the heart of winter, when everything is bare and dry. And our Lord himself is said to be "a root out of a dry ground," that, indeed, from which all the blossoms of hope and joy are to come, but which must first be owned in its own nakedness before they shall appear. If then, brethren, men have begun to fancy that their gladness has another root than this, it is meet that for a time they should be left to try whether they can keep it alive by any efforts and skill of theirs.

If Christmas joy has been separated from Christ, it is no wonder and no dishonour to Christ that it should grow feeble and hollow. But Christmas is not dead because the mirth of those who have forgotten its meaning is dead. It is not dead for you. It is not dead for people who lie upon beds tormented with fevers, dropsies, and cancers. It is not dead for the children in factories, and for the men who are working in mines, and for prisoners who never see the light of the sun. To all these the news, "The Word who was in the beginning with God and was God, in whom is life, and whose life is the light of men, by whom all things were made, and without whom was not anything made that was made, became flesh and dwelt among us, entered into our poverty, and suffering, and death"—is just as mighty and cheering news now as it was when Saint Peter first declared it to his countrymen on the day of Pentecost.

You want this truth, brethren. You cannot live or die without it. You have a right to it, no men can have a greater. By your baptism God has given you a portion in him who was made flesh; by your suffering he is inviting you to claim that portion, to understand that it is indeed for you. Christ lived and died. You may live as if no such news as this had ever been proclaimed in the world, but it is not the less true that it has been proclaimed, and proclaimed, for you. And blessed be God, this proclamation is not made merely through weak, mortal lips; that altar bears a more deep and amazing witness of it than it is possible for these words of mine to bear.

There you may learn how real the union is which the living Word of God established with the flesh of man; how truly that flesh is given to be the life of the world. Christmas day declares that he dwelt among us. To those who there eat his flesh and drink his blood, he promises that he will dwell *in* them, and that they shall dwell in him. This is the festival which makes us know, indeed, that we are members of one body; it binds together the life of Christ on earth with his life in heaven; it assures us that Christmas day belongs not to time but to eternity.

Christmas Day is more than the time for a yearly gathering with our friends and family. It is indeed the commemoration of the birth of our Lord and Savior, Jesus Christ, who was "the Word made flesh," or God Incarnate.

The Establishment of a Brotherhood

Adapted from a sermon by F. W. Robertson (1816–1853)

After Jesus was born in Bethlehem in Judea, during the time of King Herod, Magi from the east came to Jerusalem and asked, "Where is the one who has been born king of the Jews? We saw his star in the east and have come to worship him."

MATTHEW 2:1-2

When the magi, the wise men from the east, followed the star and traveled to Bethlehem, what they found was a King. There is something very telling in the fact of this King being discovered as a child. The royal child was the answer to their desires.

There are two kinds of monarchy, rule, or command. One is that of hereditary title; the other is that of divine right. There are kings of men's making, and kings of God's making. The secret of that command which men obey involuntarily is submission of the ruler himself to law. And this is the secret of the royalty of the humanity of Christ. No principle through all his life is more striking, none characterizes it so peculiarly, as his submission to another will.

"I came not to do mine own will, but the will of him

that sent me," Jesus said. "The words which I speak, I speak not of myself."

His commands are not arbitrary. They are not laws given on authority only. They are the eternal laws of our humanity, to which he himself submitted: obedience to which alone can make our being attain its end. This is the secret of his kingship—he became obedient . . . . wherefore God also hath highly exalted him. And this is the secret of all influence and all command. Obedience to a law above you subjugates minds to you who never would have yielded to mere will. "Rule thyself, thou rulest all."

We should notice the adoration of the Magians—very touching, and full of deep truth. The wisest of the world bending before the *child.* Remember the history of Magianism. It began with awe, entering into this world beneath the serene skies of the East; in wonder and worship. It passed into priestcraft and skepticism. It ended in wonder and adoration as it had begun: only with a truer and nobler meaning.

This is but a representation of human life. "Heaven lies around us in our infancy." The child looks on this world of God's as *one,* not many—all beautiful—wonderful—God's—the creation of a Father's hand. The man dissects, breaks it into fragments—loses love and worship in speculation and reasoning—becomes more manly, more independent, and less irradiated with a sense of the presence of the Lord of all; till at last, after many a devious wandering, if he be one whom the star of God is leading blind by a way he knows not, he begins to see all as one again, and God in all. Back comes the child-like spirit once more in the Christianity of old age. We kneel before the child—we feel that to adore is greater than to reason—that to love, and worship, and believe, bring the soul nearer heaven than scientific analysis. The child is nearer God than we.

And this, too, is one of the deep sayings of Christ—"Except ye be converted, and become as little children, ye shall not enter into the kingdom of heaven."

In that Epiphany we see the Magians' joy. They had seen the star in the east. They followed it—it seemed to go out in dim obscurity. They went about inquiring: asking Herod, who could tell them nothing: asking the scribes, who only gave them a vague direction. At last the star shone out once more, clear before them in their path. "When they saw the star, they rejoiced with exceeding great joy."

Perhaps the hearts of some of us can interpret that. There are some who have seen the star that shone in earlier days go out; quench itself in black vapors or sour smoke. There are some who have followed many a star that turned out to be but an *ignis fatuus*—one of those bright exhalations which hover over marshes and churchyards, and only lead to the chambers of the dead, or the cold, damp pits of disappointment: and oh, the blessing "exceeding joy," after following in vain—after inquiring of the great men and learning nothing—of the religious men and finding little—to see the star at last resting over "the place where the young child lies"—after groping the way alone, to see the star stand still—to find that religion is a thing far simpler than we thought—that God is near us—that to kneel and adore is the noblest posture of the soul. For, whoever will follow with fidelity his *own* star, God will guide him aright.

He spoke to the Magians by the star; to the shepherds by the melody of the heavenly host; to Joseph by a dream; to Simeon by an inward revelation. "Gold, and frankincense, and myrrh"—these, and ten times these, were poor and cheap to give for that blessed certainty that the star of God is on before us.

That star is now looking down on the wise men's graves; and if there be no life to come, then this is the confusion: that mass of inert matter is pursuing its way through space, and the minds that watched it, calculated its movements, were led by it through aspiring wishes to holy adorations; those minds, more precious than a thousand stars, have dropped out of God's universe.

And then God cares for mere material masses more than for spirits, which are the emanation and copy of himself. Impossible! "God is not the God of the dead, but of the living." God is the Father of our *spirits.* Eternity and immeasurableness belong to thought alone. You may measure the cycles of that star by years and miles: can you bring any measurement which belongs to time or space, by which you can compute the length or breadth or the duration of one pure thought, one aspiration, one moment of love? This is eternity. Nothing but thought can be immortal.

Learn the truth of the Epiphany by heart. To the Jew it chiefly meant that the Gentile too could become the child of God. But to us; is that doctrine obsolete? Nay, it requires to be reiterated in this age as much as in any other. There is a spirit in all our hearts whereby we would monopolize God, conceiving of him as an unapproachable being; whereby we may terrify other men outside our own pale, instead of as the

Father that is near to all, whom we may approach, and whom to adore is blessedness.

Jesus Christ has come to break down the wall of partition between us and God and to become our heavenly Father. There is now no distinction in the spiritual family between Jew, Greek, Roman, or any other group, only a true and real brotherhood on earth.

A Glorious—and Humble—Announcement

Adapted from the works of Origen of Alexandria (185–254)

The Lord Jesus Christ has been born, and an angel has come down from heaven to announce his birth. But let us see whom the angel sought out to announce his coming. He did not go to Jerusalem. He did not seek out Scribes and Pharisees. He did not enter a synagogue of the Jews. Instead, he found "shepherds in the fields keeping watch over their flock" and said to them, "Today a Savior is born for you, who is Christ the Lord."

Do you think that the words of the Scriptures signify nothing else, nothing more divine, but only say this, that an angel came to shepherds and spoke to them? Listen, shepherds of the churches! Listen, God's shepherds! His angel always comes down from heaven and proclaims to you, "Today a Savior is born for you, who is Christ the Lord." For, unless that Shepherd comes, the shepherds of the churches will be unable to guard the flock well. Their custody is weak, unless Christ pastures and guards it along with them.

We just read from the apostle Paul, "We are God's fellow workers" (1 Corinthians 3:9). A good shepherd, who imitates *the* Good Shepherd, is a coworker with God and

Christ. He is a good shepherd precisely because he has the best Shepherd with him, pasturing his sheep along with him. For, "God established in his Church apostles, prophets, evangelists, shepherds, and teachers. He established for the perfection of the saints."

But we should ascend to a more hidden understanding. Some shepherds were angels that governed human affairs. Each of these kept his watch. They were vigilant day and night.

But, at some point, they were unable to bear the labor of the peoples who had been entrusted to them and accomplish it diligently. When the Lord was born, an angel came and announced to the shepherds that the true Shepherd appeared. Let me give an example. There was a certain angel in Macedonia who needed the Lord's help. Consequently, he appeared to Paul in his dreams as a Macedonian man "and said, 'Cross over to Macedonia and help us.'" Why do I speak of Paul, since the angel said this not to Paul but Jesus, who was in Paul? So shepherds need the presence of Christ. For this reason, an angel came down from heaven said, "Do not fear. For behold, I announce great joy to you."

It was indeed a great joy to these shepherds, to whom care of men and provinces had been entrusted, that Christ had come into the world. The angel who administered affairs of Egypt received a considerable advantage after the Lord came down from heaven, for the Egyptians could become Christians. It profited all who governed the various: for example, the guardian of Macedonia, the guardian of Achaea, and the guardians of the other regions. It is right to believe that wicked angels govern individual and good angels do not have the same regions entrusted to them. I think that what is written in Scripture about individual provinces should also be believed more about all people. Two angels attend each human being. One is an angel of justice, the other an angel of iniquity. If good thoughts are present in our hearts and justice springs up in our souls, the angel of the Lord is undoubtedly speaking to us. But, if evil thoughts turn over in our hearts, the devil's angel is speaking to us. Just as there are two angels for individuals, so, I believe, there are different angels in individual provinces, some good and some evil.

For example, very wicked angels kept watch over Ephesus, on account of the sinners who lived in that city. But, because there were many believers in that city, there was also a good angel for the church of the Ephesians. What we have said about Ephesus should be applied to all the provinces. Before the coming of the Lord and Savior, those angels could bring little benefit to those entrusted to them, and their efforts were not powerful enough to bring about success. What indicates that they were hardly able to help those under their charge? Listen to what we say. When the angel of the Egyptians was helping the Egyptians, hardly one proselyte came to believe in God. And this took place when an angel was administering to the Egyptians.

But then many proselytes among the Egyptians and the Idumaeans received faith in God. That is why Scripture says, "You shall not detest the Egyptian, because you were strangers in the land of Egypt. Nor shall you despise the Idumaean, because he is your brother. If sons are born to them, they will enter the Church of God in the third generation." And thus it happened. From every nation some became proselytes. The angels, who had these nations subject to them, strove to attain this. Now nations of believers come to faith in Jesus. The angels to whom the churches have been entrusted have been strengthened by the presence of the Savior and bring in many proselytes.

Assemblies of Christians come together throughout the whole world. For this reason, let us rise up and praise the Lord. Let us become a spiritual Israel in place of the carnal Israel. Let us bless Almighty God by deed and thought and word in Christ Jesus, to whom is glory and power for ages of ages. Amen.

God chose to announce the birth of his Son to the most humble—some lowly shepherds doing nothing but what they did night after night—so that he could set an example of humility for those who would proclaim the name of Jesus Christ.

NATIVITY SEVEN

Celebrate and Share the Good News of Christ's Birth

The Sages and the Star

Adapted from the writings of Joseph Hall (1574–1656)

Then Herod called the Magi secretly and found out from them the exact time the star had appeared. He sent them to Bethlehem and said, "Go and make a careful search for the child. As soon as you find him, report to me, so that I too may go and worship him." After they had heard the king, they went on their way, and the star they had seen in the east went ahead of them until it stopped over the place where the child was. When they saw the star, they were overjoyed. On coming to the house, they saw the child with his mother Mary, and they bowed down and worshiped him. Then they opened their treasures and presented him with gifts of gold and of incense and of myrrh.

MATTHEW 2:7-11

The Magi—the wise men from the east who had traveled many days to worship the newborn King of the Jews—are on their way from Jerusalem to Bethlehem. They are full of expectation and desire, and apparently no one from Jerusalem or from King Herod's court travels with them.

Whether distrust or fear hindered them, I don't know. But of so many thousands of Jews in the Holy City, no one stirs his foot to go and see that King of theirs, the King these strangers have come so far to visit. Yet were these resolute sages discouraged with this solitariness and small respect, or drawn to repent of their journey, as thinking, *What, do we come so far to honor a King whom no man will acknowledge? What mean we to travel so many hundred miles to see that which the inhabitants will not look out to behold?* No, they cheerfully renew their journey to that place which the ancient light of prophecy had designed. And now behold, God encourages their holy forwardness from heaven, by sending them their first guide; as if he had said.

What need ye care for the neglect of men, when ye see heaven honors the King whom ye seek? What joy these sages conceived, when their eyes first beheld the reappearance of that happy star, they only can tell, that, after a long and sad night of temptation, they have seen the loving countenance of God shining forth upon their souls. If with obedience and courage we can follow the calling of God, in difficult enterprises, we shall not want supplies of comfort. Let not us be wanting to God, we shall be sure he cannot be wanting to us.

He who led the children of Israel by a pillar of fire into the land of promise, leads the wise men by a star to the promised seed. All his directions partake of that light which is in him: for God is light. This star moves both slowly and low, as might be fittest for the pace, for the purpose of these pilgrims. It is the goodness of God, that, in those means wherein we cannot reach him, he descends unto us. Surely when the wise men saw the star stand still, they looked about to see what palace there might be near unto that station, fit for the birth of a king; neither could they think that sorry shed was it which the star meant to point out; but finding their guide settled over that base roof, they go in to see what guest it held.

They enter, and, O God, what a King do they find! How poor! How contemptible! Wrapped in clothes, laid in straw, cradled in the manger, attended with beasts! What a sight was this, after all the glorious promises of that star, after the predictions of prophets, after the magnificence of their expectations! All their way afforded nothing so despicable as that Babe whom they came to worship.

But as those who could not have been wise men, unless they had known that the greatest glories have arisen from mean beginnings, they fall down and worship that hidden Majesty. This baseness hath bred wonder in them, not contempt: they well knew the star could not lie. They, which saw his star afar off in the east, when he lay swaddled in Bethlehem, do also see his royalty further off, in the despised state of his infancy; a royalty more than human. They well knew, that stars did not use to attend earthly kings; and if their aim had not been higher, what was a Jewish king to Persian strangers?

Answerable therefore hereunto was their adoration. Neither did they lift up empty hands to him whom they worshipped, but presented him with the most precious commodities of their country—gold, incense, myrrh—not as thinking to enrich him with these, but, by way of homage, acknowledging him the Lord of these. If these sages had been kings, and had offered a princely weight of gold, the blessed Virgin had not needed, in her purification, to have offered two young pigeons, as the sign of her penury. As God loves not empty hands, so he measures fullness by the affection.

Let it be gold, or incense, or myrrh, that we offer him, it cannot but please him, who doth not use to ask how much, but how good.

The Magi still stand today as examples of those who gave the newborn King of the Jews the very best they had to offer. Seeing that example, we can't help but do the very same.

Our Own Gold, Frankincense and Myrrh

Adapted from a sermon by Charles E. Jefferson (1860–1937)

After Jesus was born in Bethlehem in Judea, during the time of King Herod, Magi from the east came to Jerusalem and asked, "Where is the one who has been born king of the Jews? We saw his star in the east and have come to worship him."

MATTHEW 2:1-2

The King the wise men from the east came to visit certainly didn't look like a king. He had none of the pomp and circumstance of kings. He wore no crown. He wielded no scepter. His robe was not purple. He didn't ride in a chariot or on a horse. No retinue of armed men followed him up and down the land.

To his contemporaries his claim to kingship seemed preposterous, and sometimes blasphemous. For he didn't hesitate to claim to be monarch in the vast realm of the spirit. One day he sketched a picture of the judgment day, and he placed himself upon the throne. He told parables that implied that the final destinies of men were in his hand. A robber in the hour of death asked to remember him when he came into his kingdom. On one of the last Sundays of his life Jesus allowed the crowd to chant around him the words of an ancient Hebrew poet: "Blessed is the King that cometh in the name of the Lord!" They called him King, and he did not rebuke them.

It was this assertion of his kingship that caused the storm to break at last on Jesus' head. The crowd that thronged the door of Pilate's courtroom shouted loud and long: "We found this man saying that he himself is Christ a King!"' Here was a charge direct and clear, which Pilate as a Roman governor was bound to take notice of. Calling Jesus aside he asked him bluntly: "Art thou a king?" And the answer the prisoner returned so awed the heart of Pilate that he scarcely knew what to do. He desired to get rid as soon as possible of a man the like of whom he had never seen before; but when he suggested granting him release, the crowd blazed with an indignation that melted down the Roman's resolution. Above the Babel of discordant shoutings came clear and strong the words: "If thou release this man, thou art not Caesar's friend; every one that maketh himself a king speaketh against Caesar!" It was this cry that broke the procurator's will. He could not in safety release a man who was claiming to be a king. Tiberius Caesar brooked no rivals. Setting the prisoner before the crowd, he exclaimed, "Behold your King!" and with one accord they screamed: "Away with him! Away with him! Crucify him!" The chief priests chimed in, saying, "We have no king but Caesar!" It was because Jesus claimed to be a King that the Jews and Romans decreed that he should die. Over his head was written in the three chief languages of the world: "Jesus of Nazareth, the King of the Jews." Jesus Christ was crucified because he claimed to be King.

The tragedy narrated in the Gospels is only the story of a tragedy continued to the present hour. Jesus still claims to be King; but now as of old Herod is enraged against him, and the multitudes shout: "We will not have this man to reign over us!" As a genial and gentle teacher, Jesus has many admirers. His teachings are extolled by all who have minds capable of appreciating high and noble thought. The whole world is glad to praise him as an ethical guide without peer. The moral precepts promulgated in the Sermon on the Mount are eulogized by men of many schools. One of his rules has been labeled "golden" by the common consent of mankind, and the picture of the Good Samaritan has been hung up as a sacred picture in the gallery of the soul of the world. The multitudes are eager to praise and honor Jesus as a teacher, a philosopher, a poet, an idealist, a reformer, a lover of humanity. They hesitate only when they are asked to crown him King.

And yet it is at this point that he is most insistent and inexorable. Obedience is the one virtue for which he contends from first to last. Without obedience he promises no man salvation. It is only the obedient heart that is able to understand his words. Men are to show their love for him by obeying him, and it is by this obedience that the world is to be redeemed. No one is permitted to count himself a disciple who is not willing to obey. This is the tone of all kings. They demand swift and absolute subjection to their will. Their will is law, and peace and prosperity are found only in obedience. Jesus stakes everything on his kingship. His whole religion is foundationed on the fact that he is King.

At Christmas we naturally think of Jesus. Which Jesus

are you going to think about? Shall it be the Jesus of picture, or the Jesus of song? The Jesus of the artists is a lovely figure to gaze upon. For centuries the multitudes have looked upon that face and are not yet wearied. The Jesus of song is still more beautiful. "How sweet the name of Jesus sounds in a believer's ear!" Jesus has been the theme of innumerable anthems, and oratories, and cantatas, and carols and all of us are ready every year to join in singing the Christmas songs. The Jesus of the biblical narrative is also entertaining. We never grow weary of hearing the story of the baby who was born in Bethlehem, and whose mother laid him in a manger.

The world has long had the Jesus of song and picture and story. Singing about Jesus is not enough, nor is looking at the pictured face of Jesus sufficient, nor is celebrating the birthday of Jesus adequate. The Jesus of God is a King, and nothing but obedience to Jesus will lift the world out of its distresses. How solemn are his words: "Not every one that says, Lord, Lord, shall enter into the kingdom of heaven. Many will say to me in that day, Lord, Lord, and then will I profess unto them, I never knew you!" He puts to us the question with which he confided his disciples in Jerusalem: "Why do ye call me Lord, do not the things which I say?" These are words we need to ponder amid the festivities of Christmas. Where is he that is born King?

The problem of our life is to bring the Herod in us into subjection to Christ the King. Herod is of the earth earthly. Herod lives solely for himself. Herod is averse to service and to sacrifice. Herod despises the way of the cross. Herod is always planning to murder Jesus. He would murder him because Jesus insists on being King. It is

God's will that Jesus should be the Ruler of our heart, and Christmas is an angel from the court of heaven sent to remind us that all who are wise lay at the feet of the King the gold and frankincense and myrrh of an obedient life.

Jesus Christ didn't come into the world—being born of a virgin and taking on the flesh of a human—to be our Savior only; he also came to be our Lord and King. We are called to trust him for our salvation, but part of our faith is obedience to his commands.

The Twofold Coming of Christ

Adapted from the writings of Cyril of Jerusalem (315–386)

We do not preach only one coming of Christ, but a second as well, much more glorious than the first. The first coming was marked by patience; the second will bring the crown of a divine kingdom.

In general, whatever relates to our Lord Jesus Christ has two aspects. There is a birth from God before the ages, and a birth from a virgin at the fullness of time. There is a hidden coming, like that of rain on fleece, and a coming before all eyes, still in the future.

At the first coming he was wrapped in swaddling clothes in a manger. At his second coming he will be clothed in light as in a garment. In the first coming he endured the cross, despising the shame; in the second coming he will be in glory, escorted by an army of angels.

We look then beyond the first coming and await the second. At the first coming we said: *Blessed is he who comes in the name of the Lord.* At the second we shall say it again; we shall go out with the angels to meet the Lord and cry out in adoration: *Blessed is he who comes in the name of the Lord.* The Savior will not come to be judged again, but to judge those by whom he was judged. At his own judgment he was silent; then he will address those who committed the outrages against him when they crucified him and will remind them: *You did these things, and I was silent.*

His first coming was to fulfill his plan of love, to teach men by gentle persuasion. This time, whether men like it or not, they will be subjects of his kingdom by necessity.

The prophet Malachi speaks of the two comings. *And the Lord whom you seek will come suddenly to his temple:* that is one coming. Again he says of another coming: *Look, the Lord almighty will come, and who will endure the day of his entry, or who will stand in his sight? Because he comes like a refiner's fire, a fuller's herb, and he will sit refining and cleansing.*

These two comings are also referred to by Paul in writing to Titus: *The grace of God the Savior has appeared to all men, instructing us to put aside impiety and worldly desires and live temperately, uprightly, and religiously in this present age, waiting for the joyful hope, the appearance of the glory of our great God and Savior, Jesus Christ.* Notice how he speaks of a first coming for which he gives thanks, and a second, the one we still await.

That is why the faith we profess has been handed on to you in these words: *He ascended into heaven, and is seated at the right hand of the Father, and he will come again in glory to judge the living and the dead, and his kingdom will have no end.*

Our Lord Jesus Christ will therefore come from heaven. He will come at the end of the world, in glory, at the last day. For there will be an end to this world, and the created world will be made new.

The birth of Jesus Christ in Bethlehem was an epic moment in the formation of the Christian faith, but we must always remember that he will one day return from heaven, not as a baby so humbly born in a manger but as the King of Kings and Lord of lords.

The Nativity

Peace? and to all the world? sure, One
And He the Prince of Peace, hath none.
He travels to be born, and then
Is born to travel more again.
Poor Galilee! thou canst not be
The place for His nativity.
His restless mother's called away,
And not delivered till she pay.

A tax? 'tis so still! we can see
The church thrive in her misery;
And like her Head at Bethelem, rise
When she, oppressed with troubles, lies.
Rise? should all fall, we cannot be
In more extremities than He.
Great Type of passions! come what will,
Thy grief exceeds all copies still.
Thou cam'st from heaven to earth, that we
Might go from earth to heaven with Thee.
And though Thou foundest no welcome here,
Thou didst provide us mansions there.
A stable was Thy court, and when
Men turned to beasts, beasts would be men.

They were Thy courtiers, others none;
And their poor manger was Thy throne.
No swaddling silks Thy limbs did fold,
Though Thou couldst turn Thy rays to gold.
No rockers waited on Thy birth,
No cradles stirred, nor songs of mirth;
But her chaste lap and sacred breast
Which lodged Thee first did give Thee rest.

But stay: what light is that doth stream,
And drop here in a gilded beam?
It is Thy star runs page, and brings
Thy tributary Eastern kings.
Lord! grant some light to us, that we
May with them find the way to Thee.
Behold what mists eclipse the day:
How dark it is! shed down one ray
To guide us out of this sad night,
And say once more, "Let there be light."

—Henry Vaughan (1621–1695)

Our Lord Jesus Christ, the One the Bible calls "the Prince of Peace," didn't enjoy peace at the beginning of his life. On the contrary, he was born under extraordinary circumstances. He also lived an extraordinary life and died an extraordinary death—all so he could bring us peace with his Father.

Shepherds and Angels

Extracted and adapted from writings of Alexander MacLaren (1826–1910)

There were shepherds living out in the fields nearby, keeping watch over their flocks at night. An angel of the Lord appeared to them, and the glory of the Lord shone around them, and they were terrified. But the angel said to them, "Do not be afraid. I bring you good news of great joy that will be for all the people. Today in the town of David a Savior has been born to you; he is Christ the Lord. This will be a sign to you: You will find a baby wrapped in cloths and lying in a manger." Suddenly a great company of the heavenly host appeared with the angel, praising God and saying, "Glory to God in the highest, and on earth peace to men on whom his favor rests."

LUKE 2:8-14

The central portion of this passage is, of course, the angels' message and song, the former of which proclaims the transcendent fact of the Incarnation, and the latter hymns its blessed results. But, subsidiary to these, the silent vision which preceded them and the visit to Bethlehem that followed are to be noted. Taken together, they cast varying gleams on the great fact of the birth of Jesus Christ.

Why should there be a miraculous announcement at all, and why should it be to these shepherds? It seems to have had no effect beyond a narrow circle and for a time. It was apparently utterly forgotten when, thirty years after, the carpenter's Son began his ministry. Could such an event have passed from memory, and left no ripple on the surface? Does the lack of results cast suspicion on the truthfulness of the narrative? Not if we duly give weight to the few who knew of the wonder; to the length of time that elapsed, during which the shepherds and their auditors probably died; to their humble position; to the short remembrance of extraordinary events that have no immediate consequences. Joseph and Mary were strangers in Bethlehem. Christ never visited it, so far as we know. The fading of the impression cannot be called strange, for it accords with natural tendencies; but the record of so great an event, which was entirely ineffectual as regards future acceptance of Christ's claims, is so unlike legend that vouches for the truth of the narrative. An apparent stumbling block is left, because the story is true.

Why then, the announcement at all, since it was of so little use? Because it was of some; but still more, because it was fitting that such angel voices should attend such an event, whether men gave heed to them or not; and because, recorded, their song has helped the world to understand the nature and meaning of birth. The glory died off the hillside quickly, and the music of the song scarcely lingered longer in the ears of its first hearers; but its notes echo still in all lands, every generation turns to them with wonder and hope.

The selection of two or three peasants as receivers of

the message, the time at which it was given, and place, are all significant. It was no unmeaning fact that the "glory of the Lord" shone lambent round the shepherds, and held them and the angel standing beside them in its circle of light. No longer within the secret shrine, but out in the open field, the symbol of the Divine Presence glowed through the darkness; for that birth hallowed common life, and brought the glory of God into familiar intercourse with its secularities and smallnesses. The appearance to these humble men as they "sat simply chatting in a rustic row" symbolized the destination of the Gospel for all ranks and classes.

The angel speaks by the side of the shepherds, not from above. His gentle encouragement, "Fear not!" not only soothes their present terror, but has a wider meaning. The dread of the Unseen, which lies coiled like a sleeping snake in all hearts, is utterly taken away by the Incarnation. All messages from that realm are thenceforward "tidings of great joy," and love and desire may pass into it, as all men shall one day pass, and both enterings may be peaceful and confident. Nothing harmful can come out of the darkness, from which Jesus has come, into which he has passed, and which he fills.

The great announcement, the mightiest, most wonderful word that had ever passed angels' immortal lips, *is* characterized as "great joy" to "all the people," in which designation two things are to be noted—the nature and the limitation of the message. In how many ways the Incarnation was to be the fountain of purest gladness was but little discerned, either by the heavenly messenger or the shepherds. The ages since have been partially learning it, but not till the glorified joy of heaven swells redeemed hearts will all its sorrow-dispelling power be experimentally known. Base joys may be basely sought, but his creatures' gladness is dear to God, and if sought in God's way, is a worthy object of their efforts.

The worldwide sweep of the Incarnation does not appear here, but only its first destination for Israel. This is manifest in the phrase "all the people," in the mention of "the city of David" and in the emphatic "you," in contradistinction both from the messenger, who announced what he did not share, and Gentiles, to whom the blessing was not to pass till Israel had determined its attitude to it.

The titles of the Infant tell something of the wonder of the birth, but do not unfold its overwhelming mystery. Magnificent as they are, they fall far short of "The Word was made flesh." They keep within the circle of Jewish expectation, and announce that the hopes of centuries are fulfilled. There is something very grand in the accumulation of titles, each greater than the preceding, and all culminating in that final "Lord." Handel has gloriously given the spirit of it in the crash of triumph with which that last word is pealed out in his oratorio.

"Savior" means far more than the shepherds knew; for it declares the Child to be the deliverer from all evil, both of sin and sorrow, and the endower with all good, both of righteousness and blessedness. The "Christ" claims that he is the fulfiller of prophecy, perfectly endowed by divine anointing for this office of prophet, priest, and king—the consummate flower of ancient revelation, greater than Moses the lawgiver, than Solomon the king, than Jonah the prophet. "The Lord" is scarcely to be taken as the ascription of divinity, but rather as a prophecy of authority and dominion, implying reverence, but not unveiling the deepest secret of the entrance of the divine Son into humanity. That remained unrevealed, for the time was not yet ripe.

The shepherds who received the announcement of the birth of their Messiah could hardly have understood the significance of everything they heard and saw that night. But we know that this was the announcement of the Good News of the gospel of Jesus Christ for every human being.

The Joy of Christ's Birthday

Adapted from the works of Saint Augustine of Hippo (354–430)

When they had seen him, they spread the word concerning what had been told them about this child, and all who heard it were amazed at what the shepherds said to them. But Mary treasured up all these things and pondered them in her heart. The shepherds returned, glorifying and praising God for all the things they had heard and seen, which were just as they had been told.

LUKE 2:17-20

Let us, then, celebrate the Lord's birthday with the full attendance and the enthusiasm that we should give it. Let men rejoice, let women rejoice. Christ was born Man; He was born of woman. Both sexes have been honored. Let him, therefore, who had been condemned before in the first man, now become a follower of the Second Man.

A woman had been the cause of our death; a woman, again, gave birth to life for us. *The likeness of sinful flesh* was born to purify the sinful flesh. For that reason do not let the flesh be found with sin, but let sin die that nature may live; for He was born without sin, that he who was with sin might be reborn.

Young men, you who lead chaste lives, who have chosen to follow Christ in a special manner, who do not seek marriage—rejoice! Not through marriage did He come to you, He in whom you have found your ideal: He wished to give you the strength to esteem lightly that through which you have come into being. You have come into being through carnal marriage, without which He came to join a spiritual marriage; and you to whom He has given a special vocation to marriage. He has enabled to spurn marriage. Thus it is that you have no desire for that by which you have been born; because more than others have you loved Him who was not born in this manner.

Rejoice, chaste virgins. A virgin has brought forth for you Him to whom you may espouse yourselves without corruption. Neither in conceiving Him nor in giving birth to Him can you destroy what you love.

Rejoice, you who are just. It is the birthday of Him who justifies.

Rejoice, you who are weak and sick. It is the birthday of Him who makes well.

Rejoice, you who are in captivity. It is the birthday of the Redeemer.

Rejoice, you who are slaves. It is the birthday of the Master.

Rejoice, you who are free. It is the birthday of Him who makes free.

Rejoice, you Christians all. It is Christ's birthday.

There is no birthday we should rejoice over and celebrate more than that of our Lord Jesus Christ. Each and every one of us who knows him—and those who need to know him—

should celebrate Christmas as far more than a nice family holiday. It is a time to celebrate the birth of the One who would change things between God and us for all time.

Herod and the Devil

Extracted and adapted from a sermon by John Knox (1505–1572)

When Herod realized that he had been outwitted by the Magi, he was furious, and he gave orders to kill all the boys in Bethlehem and its vicinity who were two years old and under, in accordance with the time he had learned from the Magi. Then what was said through the prophet Jeremiah was fulfilled: "A voice is heard in Ramah, weeping and great mourning, Rachel weeping for her children and refusing to be comforted, because they are no more."

MATTHEW 2:16-18

How Satan raged at the tidings of Christ's nativity! What blood he caused to be shed on purpose to have murdered Christ in His infancy! The evangelist Saint Matthew witnesses that in all the coasts and borders of Bethlehem the children of two years old and less age were murdered without mercy. A fearful spectacle and horrid example of insolent and unaccustomed tyranny!

And what is the cause moving Satan thus to rage against innocents, considering that by reason of their imperfections they could not hurt his kingdom at that instant? Oh, the crafty eye of Satan looked farther than to the present time;

he heard reports by the wise men, that they had learned by the appearance of a star that the King of the Jews was born; and he was not ignorant that the time prophesied of Christ's coming was then instant; for a stranger was clad with the crown and scepter of Judah.

The angel had declared the glad tidings to the shepherds, that a Savior, which was Christ the Lord, was born in the city of David. All these tidings inflamed the wrath and malice of Satan, for he perfectly understood that the coming of the promised Seed was appointed to his confusion, and to the breaking down of his head and tyranny; and therefore he raged most cruelly, even at the first hearing of Christ's birth, thinking that although he could not hinder nor withstand His coming, yet he could shorten his days upon earth, lest by long life and peaceable quietness in it, the number of good men, by Christ's doctrine and virtuous life, should be multiplied; and so he strove to cut Him away among the other children before He could open His mouth on His Father's message. Oh, cruel serpent! In vain dost thou spend thy venom, for the days of God's elect thou canst not shorten! And when the wheat is fallen on the ground, then doth it most multiply.

But from these things mark, what has been the practice of the devil from the beginning—most cruelly to rage against God's children when God begins to show them His mercy. And, therefore, marvel not, dearly beloved, although the like come unto you. If Satan fume or roar against you, whether it be against your bodies by persecution, or inwardly in your conscience by a spiritual battle, be not discouraged, as though you were less acceptable in

God's presence, or as if Satan might at any time prevail against you.

No; your temptations and storms, that arise so suddenly, argue and witness that the seed which is sown is fallen on good ground, begins to take root and shall, by God's grace, bring forth fruit abundantly in due season and convenient time. That is it which Satan fears, and therefore thus he rages, and shall rage against you, thinking that if he can repulse you now suddenly in the beginning, that then you shall be at all times an easy prey, never able to resist his assaults. But as my hope is good, so shall my prayer be, that so you may be strengthened, that the world and Satan himself may perceive or understand that God fights your battle.

The birth of Jesus was an event that heralded "good will toward men," meaning that God was about to pour out his blessing and mercy on all humankind through the birth of his only begotten Son, Jesus Christ. This event was a blessing to us and the death knell for the enemy of our souls, the devil.

Mary

Adapted from a sermon by Phillips Brooks (1835–1893)

In the sixth month, God sent the angel Gabriel to Nazareth, a town in Galilee, to a virgin pledged to be married to a man named Joseph, a descendant of David. The virgin's name was Mary. The angel went to her and said, "Greetings, you who are highly favored! The Lord is with you."

LUKE 1:26-28

Who are the first group, then, that are concerned in the Nativity that are gathered about the birth of Jesus? Certainly those who stood the nearest to Him. Certainly His parents, and especially His mother, who had borne already so long upon her heart the coming mystery. What was the nativity to her whom all generations have called blessed as the mother of our Lord? What should we see if we could look into her heart on Christmas Day?

Painters, you know, have tried to tell the story in exquisite pictures, which represent the mother on her knees before her Child, who lies before her. She is wrapt in adoration of Him; she is lifting up her hands in homage; she is imploring His blessing and owning Him for her Lord. But while that is what art has seized upon, it is remarkable that there is not one word about that in the Bible. There we have one key to the mother's heart: we have the beautiful psalm, the Magnificat, which she sang when she went to visit Elizabeth before the Savior's birth. And it is certainly noticeable that that psalm is mainly of her own privilege: "He hath regarded the low estate of his handmaiden: for . . . from henceforth all generations shall call me blessed. . . . He that is mighty hath done to me great things" (Luke 1:48-49, KJV). It is not adoration of her Child. It is a sense of what that Child's coming has been to her. Because He has deigned to be born of her she is forever blessed. Because of this close union between His life and hers she is lifted up out of her insignificance. Because He has shared her lot, her lot has ceased to be mean and wretched. She is sacred because of the God who has come and lived in her life. The poor Jewish girl is not despicable, no one shall despise her, she never will despise herself again, now that her life has been capable of containing the very life of God.

Afterward, no doubt, there came the adoration. Afterward, as Christ grew and she knew Him more, there came forth in Him a Divinity that she could not share, before which she could only stand in loving awe. Afterward she saw how different He was from her. But at first the thought is of how they are one with each other, and of how by her oneness with Him she is lifted and glorified. At first it is not the sense of how far His Divinity is above her, but of how truly it is in her and how it makes her divine. On Christmas Day she is not on her knees before her Lord, but she is holding her Child tight to her heart to assure herself continually that His life is really hers, and so that her life is really His.

Now extend all this—make it not merely the experience of the Jewish virgin, but the consciousness of humanity at the birth of Jesus—and we have this, which I hold to be true: that the first thing which human nature feels when it comes to the knowledge of the coming of Christ is the mere fact of the Incarnation, and the illumination and exaltation of all human life by and through the Incarnation. With her it was a feeling of personal pride and privilege. Out of all the maidens of Judah she had been chosen to be the mother of the Lord. But with men to whom the same truth comes in its larger way its narrowness is lost; it becomes comprehensive; it is a sense of the exaltation and illumination of all humanity together, and of each man only as he has a part in that humanity by the coming of God into its flesh.

Carry this out into a slight detail with regard to the life of Mary. As Christ grew older this first feeling must have grown only stronger with her. In everything her life must have been elevated by seeing how her Son could share it with her. Her humble house must have seemed glorious, her simple meal a banquet, her husband's workshop sacred, the ordinary household thoughts not commonplace, because they were not hers alone, but His. That must have been the first power of the Incarnation. Only after that was fully felt could the second power of the Incarnation be experienced. Only after she had thoroughly conceived the dignity of her daily tasks when Christ took part in them could she begin to perceive how differently He did them from the way in which she did them, and so learn how her actual life fell short of the dignity with which the revelation of His birth had vested it. The Incarnation must have stirred her pride before it stirred her shame.

So it ought to be with us. So the first simple, broad, pervading sentiment of Christmas Day ought to be of how sacred and high this human life is into which the Lord was born. Not merely the body and the life of the virgin—she was like all her brethren and sisters. All attempts to separate her from them is a wrong to their common humanity. But the body and the life of man are able to take in and to utter God. Christ could be born into such flesh and such relationships, into such duties and such delights, as ours. At once a radiance streams in upon them and they are no longer dull. Their luster shines out splendidly. Fathers, your labor for your children is not bare duty. Children, your service of your fathers is not a weary slavery. Neighbors, your daily courtesies to one another need not be empty shams. Men and women, your bodies are not base, your routines ought not to be deadening. Each is worthy of his own and of his brethren's respect; for there has been an incarnation. This humanity has held Divinity. God has been in this flesh.

When our lives are hampered and held down by self-contempt, by feelings that human life is worthless, that to be human is to be something narrow, dry, and barren; when any such thoughts keep us from doing broad justice to ourselves and to our brethren, we should cast them aside on Christmas Day. Instead, let us believe that Christ was born of Mary. Let our souls magnify the Lord with the same bounding and leaping sense of privilege that exalted hers. Let the Incarnation, with all its inspirations and its shames, possess and fill our lives.

Sources

Nativity 1: God's Loving Gift

"In the Bleak Midwinter," by Christina Rossetti (1830–1882).

"Christ's Nativity: God's Gift Just for Us." Adapted from a sermon by John Wycliffe (1324–1384). *20 Centuries of Great Preaching* (Waco, TX: Word Books, 1971).

"On the Morning of Christ's Nativity," by John Milton (1608–1674). Al Bryant, *Sourcebook of Poetry* (Grand Rapids, MI: Zondervan Publishing House, 1968).

"Our Savior's Humble Birth." Adapted from a sermon by the Reverend Alfred Barratt. Rev. G. B. F. Hallock, ed. *One Hundred Best Sermons for Special Occasions* (New York: Richard. R. Smith, Inc., 1930).

"Keeping Christmas," by Henry van Dyke (1852–1933).

"The Joy of the Nativity." Based on a sermon by Saint Augustine of Hippo (354–430). *20 Centuries of Great Preaching* (Waco, TX: Word Books, 1971).

"The Three Kings," by Henry Wadsworth Longfellow (1807–1882).

"Proclaiming God's Greatness." Adapted from the writings of Bede the Venerable (673–735).

"The Story behind 'Silent Night.'" Ernest K. Emurian, *Living Stories of Famous Hymns* (Grand Rapids, MI: Baker Book House, 1955).

"From Starry Heav'n Descending," by J. R. Newell.

Nativity 2: The Word Became Flesh

"God with Us." Adapted from a sermon by Edward Bouverie Pusey (1800–1882).

"Inspired by What He Saw," based on the hymn "O Little Town of Bethlehem." Adapted from various sources, but writing is original.

"The Nativity: When the Word Became Flesh." Adapted from a sermon by Saint John of Kronstadt (1829–1908). G. Spruksts, trans. *Solntse Pravdy: O Zhizni i Uchenii Gospoda Nashego, Iisusa Khrista* [The Sun of Righteousness: On the Life and Teaching of Our Lord, Jesus Christ]. English-language translation copyright © 1983, 1996 by The Saint Stefan of Perm' Guild, The Russian Cultural Heritage Society, and the Translator. All rights reserved. Reprinted by permission from *KITEZH: The Journal of the Russian Cultural Heritage Society*, Vol. 12, No. 4 (48).

"God with Us!" by Charles H. Spurgeon (1834–1892). *Morning and Evening.*

"The Wonder of Christ's Nativity." Adapted from the writings of Gregory of Neocaesarea (213–270).

"A Christmas Carol," by Samuel Taylor Coleridge (1777–1834). Al Bryant, *Sourcebook of Poetry* (Grand Rapids, MI: Zondervan Publishing House, 1968).

"The Light of the World," by Evelyn Underhill (1875–1941). *Watch for the Night: Readings for Advent and Christmas.*

"Born to Save!" Adapted from the writings of Athanasius the Great (298–373). *On the Incarnation* (St. Vladimir's Seminary Press, New Ed edition, June 1975).

"Some Christmas Poetry," by George Herbert (1593–1633).

"The Birthday of Life." Adapted from a sermon by Leo the Great (fifth century).

Nativity 3: Christ Our Substitute

"On the Night of Nativity." Adapted from the writings of Ephraim the Syrian (306–373).

"Carol," by Ben Jonson (1572–1637).

"True Way of Keeping Christmas." Excerpted and adapted from a sermon by George Whitefield (1714–1770).

"The Completeness of the Substitution." Adapted from *The Everlasting Righteousness,* by Horatius Bonar (1808–1889).

"All for Our Sake." Adapted from ancient Syriac liturgy.

"No Room in the Inn." Adapted from the works of Charles H. Spurgeon (1834–1892).

"To You Christ Is Born." Excerpted and adapted from a 1530 Christmas sermon by Martin Luther (1483–1546).

"On the Birthday of Christ." Excerpted and adapted from a sermon by Gregory Nazianzus (Gregory the Theologian, 329–389).

"The Mystery of God's Loving-kindness." Excerpted and adapted from a sermon by Saint John of Kronstadt (1829–1908). G. Spruksts, trans. *Taina miloserdiya: slovo na dyen' Rozhdestva Khristova* [The Mystery Of Loving-kindness: A Sermon for the Day of Christ's Nativity]. English-language translation copyright © 1999 by The St. Stefan of Perm' Guild, The Russian Cultural Heritage Society, and the Translator. All rights reserved.

"To the Birth of Jesus." Excerpted from the works of Saint Teresa of Avila (1515–1582). Kieran Kavanaugh, O.C.D., and Otilio Rodriguez, O.C.D., trans. *The Collected Works of St. Teresa of Avila* (Vol. III) (ICS Publications, 1985).

Nativity 4: Prayers of Thanks and Praise for the Nativity

"Classic Prayers for the Nativity." From several public domain sources.

"Calm on the Listening Ear of Night," by Edmund Hamilton Sears (1810–1876).

"The Joy of the Nativity." Adapted from a sermon by Saint Bernard of Clairvaux (1090–1153). St. Mary's Convent, trans. and ed. *Sermons of St. Bernard on Advent and Christmas* (Benziger Brothers, printers to the Holy Apostolic See, 1909).

"The Precious, Sweet Name of Jesus." Adapted from a sermon by Charles H. Spurgeon (1834–1892).

"Nativity Poem from 'At Sundown'" by John Greenleaf Whittier (1807–1892).

"Wise Men Seek Him." Adapted from *Matthew Henry Commentary on the Whole Bible,* by Matthew Henry (1666–1714).

"Hymn for the Nativity" by Edward Thring (1821–1887). *Poems and Translations* (1887).

"Christ in Me." Adapted from *The Spirit of Prayer,* by William Law (1686–1761).

"Christ's Nativity," by Henry Vaughan (1621–1695).

Nativity 5: The Birth of Jesus Fulfills the Promises of God

"Christ's Birth: Promises Fulfilled." Adapted from the works of Irenaeus of Lyons (115–202). Johannes Quasten, S.T.D. and Joseph C. Plumpe, Ph.D., eds. *Ancient Christian Writers: The Works of the Fathers in Translation* (New York: Newman Press, 1952).

"The Birth of Our Mediator." Adapted from a sermon by John Calvin (1509–1564). *Calvin's Sermons: The Deity of Christ and Other Sermons* (Grand Rapids, MI: Eerdman's Publishing Co., 1950).

"Born to Conquer Death." Adapted from a sermon by Dwight L. Moody (1837–1899). *New Sermons, Addresses and Prayers by Dwight Lyman Moody* (Philadelphia, PA: F. Scofield & Co. Publishers, 1877).

"A Christmas without Christ," by Clovis G. Chappell (1881–1972). *Chappell's Special Day Sermons* (Nashville: Cokesbury Press, 1936).

"The Profound Miracle of Christ's Birth." Adapted from the works of Peter Chrysologus (406–450). William B. Parlardy, trans. *The Fathers of the Church: A New Translation* (Washington, D.C.: The Catholic University of America Press, 2005).

"The Sign Is a Baby," by E. Stanley Jones (1884–1973). *Victorious Living* (New York: Abingdon Press, 1936).

"Entering in at the Lowly Doors," by John Henry Jowett (1864–1923). *My Daily Meditation* (New York: Fleming H. Revell Co., 1914).

"The Wonder of His Name," by Francis Ridley Havergal (1836–1879). William J. Pell, ed. *Open Treasures* (New York: Loizeaux Bros., 1962).

Nativity 6: Humble Beginnings to Reach All of Humanity

"The Creator of the Universe . . . Surrounded by Mud and Clay." Excerpted and adapted from a sermon by Saint Jerome (341–420).

"Mary and Elizabeth." Adapted from the writings of Ambrose of Milan (340–397).

"The Angels' Christmas Message: Do Not Be Afraid!" Adapted from a sermon by Theodore Christlieb (1833–1889). Wilbur R. Smith, ed. *Great Sermons on the Birth of Christ* (W. A. Wilde Company, 1963).

"Joseph." Adapted from the writings of Alexander Whyte (1837–1921). *The Nature of Angels. Eight Addresses by Alexander Whyte* (Grand Rapids, MI: Baker Book House, 1930).

"Good News from Bethlehem." Adapted from the works of Horatius Bonar (1808–1889). *Christ the Healer* (Grand Rapids, MI: Baker Book House, 1977).

"Wonderful." Adapted from a work by Billy Sunday (1862–1935).

"Christmas Day: A Taste of Eternity." Adapted from the works of Frederick Denison Maurice (1805–1872). *Christmas Day and Other Sermons* (New York: MacMillan & Co., 1892).

"The Establishment of a Brotherhood." Adapted from a sermon by F. W. Robertson (1816–1853). *The Preaching of F. W. Robertson* (Philadelphia: Fortress Press, 1964).

"A Glorious—and Humble—Announcement." Adapted from the works of Origen of Alexandria (185–254). Johannes Quasten, S.T.D., and Joseph C. Plumpe, Ph.D., eds. *Ancient Christian Writers: The Works of the Fathers in Translation* (New York: Newman Press, 1952).

Nativity 7: Celebrate and Share the Good News of Christ's Birth

"The Sages and the Star." Adapted from *Contemplations of the Historical Passages of the Old and New Testaments,* by Joseph Hall (1574–1656).

"Our Own Gold, Frankincense and Myrrh." Adapted from a sermon by Charles E. Jefferson (1860-1937). Rev. G. B. F. Hallock, ed. *One Hundred Best Sermons for Special Occasions* (New York: Richard. R. Smith, Inc., 1930).

"The Twofold Coming of Christ." Adapted from the writings of Cyril of Jerusalem (315–386).

"The Nativity," by Henry Vaughan (1621–1695).

"Shepherds and Angels." Extracted and adapted from the writings of Alexander MacLaren (1826–1910). *Expositions of the Holy Scripture* (Hartford, CT: The S. S. Scranton Company).

"The Joy of Christ's Birthday." Adapted from the works of Saint Augustine of Hippo (354–430). Johannes Quasten, S.T.D., and Joseph C. Plumpe, Ph.D., eds. *Ancient Christian Writers: The Works of the Fathers in Translation* (New York: Newman Press, 1952).

"Herod and the Devil." Extracted and adapted from a sermon by John Knox (1505–1572). Grenville Kleiser, ed. *The World's Great Sermons* (Vol. 1) (Funk and Wagnalls Company, 1909).

"Mary." Adapted from a sermon by Phillips Brooks (1835–1893). *Sermons: For the Principal Festivals and Fasts of the Church Year,* 7th ser. (New York: E. P. Dutton & Co., 1895).

Index of Names

About the Author

James Stuart Bell is presently the owner of Whitestone Communications, a literary development agency. He consults with numerous publishers, represents various authors, and provides writing and editing services. He has previously served as executive editor at Moody Press, director of religious publishing at Doubleday, and publisher at Bridge Publishing.

As general manager of the Princeton Religion Research Center, he worked with George Gallup Jr. in polling Americans concerning their religious beliefs and practices. His own clients in that area include major denominations, parachurch organizations, political groups, and television networks. He has received cover credit on over forty titles. These include Christian classics, prayer books, devotionals, works of fiction, and study guides.

He has co-authored the best-selling *Complete Idiot's Guide to the Bible,* with over 300,000 sold, and numerous other Christian guides in that series for Penguin Group. He has also contributed numerous volumes to the best-selling Cup of Comfort series by Adams Media.

Other Nativity books from Tyndale

The Nativity Story—A novelization of the major motion picture. Best-selling author Angela Hunt presents a heartwarming adaptation of *The Nativity Story*. Hunt brings the story of Christ's birth to life with remarkable attention to detail and a painstaking commitment to historical accuracy.

Also available in Spanish.

Other Nativity books from Tyndale

Why the Nativity?—Why Bethlehem? Why Jesus? Why did God send his only Son to earth as a baby? In response to *The Nativity Story* movie release, David Jeremiah, in his hallmark style, explains for believers and skeptics alike why it is important to examine again the birth of Jesus.

Also available in Spanish.

Other Nativity books from Tyndale

A Classic Nativity Devotional— The Nativity is one of the most vibrant traditions we celebrate today. This Christmas, experience the wonder and awe of the season through the poetry and prose of such classic authors as Martin Luther, Charles Spurgeon, John Milton, Christina Rossetti, Henry Wadsworth Longfellow, and many others.

Looking Forward to the Nativity— Twenty-five daily devotions bring the true meaning of Christmas home this season. Written with families in mind, each devotion is accompanied by a family-friendly activity designed to help your children understand how the baby Jesus fulfilled everything God had promised from the beginning.

Available now in stores and online!